HAY HOUSE BASICS
CRYSTALS

❖ Also in the Hay House Basics series ❖

Angels

Mindfulness

Past Lives

Coming soon

Lucid Dreaming

Tarot

Energy Healing

Self-Hypnosis

NLP

Reiki

Numerology

CRYSTALS

How to Use Crystals and Their Energy to Enhance Your Life

JUDY HALL

HAY
HOUSE

HAY HOUSE

Carlsbad, California • New York City • London • Sydney
Johannesburg • Vancouver • Hong Kong • New Delhi

First published and distributed in the United Kingdom by:
Hay House UK Ltd, Astley House, 33 Notting Hill Gate, London W11 3JQ
Tel: +44 (0)20 3675 2450; Fax: +44 (0)20 3675 2451; www.hayhouse.co.uk

Published and distributed in the United States of America by:
Hay House Inc., PO Box 5100, Carlsbad, CA 92018-5100
Tel: (1) 760 431 7695 or (800) 654 5126; Fax: (1) 760 431 6948 or (800) 650 5115
www.hayhouse.com

Published and distributed in Australia by:
Hay House Australia Ltd, 18/36 Ralph St, Alexandria NSW 2015
Tel: (61) 2 9669 4299; Fax: (61) 2 9669 4144; www.hayhouse.com.au

Published and distributed in the Republic of South Africa by:
Hay House SA (Pty) Ltd, PO Box 990, Witkoppen 2068
Tel/Fax: (27) 11 467 8904
www.hayhouse.co.za

Published and distributed in India by:
Hay House Publishers India, Muskaan Complex, Plot No.3, B-2,
Vasant Kunj, New Delhi 110 070
Tel: (91) 11 4176 1620; Fax: (91) 11 4176 1630; www.hayhouse.co.in

Distributed in Canada by:
Raincoast Books, 2440 Viking Way, Richmond, B.C. V6V 1N2
Tel: (1) 604 448 7100; Fax: (1) 604 270 7161; www.raincoast.com

No medical claims are made for the stones in this book and the information
given is not intended to act as a substitute for medical treatment. If in any
doubt about their use, consult a qualified crystal-healing practitioner. In
the context of crystal healing, illness is a dis-ease, the final manifestation of
spiritual, environmental, psychological, karmic, emotional or mental imbalance
or distress. Healing means bringing mind, body and spirit back into balance
and facilitating evolution for the soul; it does not imply a cure. In accordance
with crystal healing consensus, all stones are referred to as crystals regardless
of whether or not they have a crystalline structure.

A catalogue record for this book is available from the British Library.

ISBN: 978-1-78180-303-5

Interior illustrations © thinkstockphotos.co.uk

'*That we find a crystal or a poppy beautiful means that we are less alone, that we are more deeply inserted into existence than the course of a single life would lead us to believe.*'

JOHN BERGER, SELECTED ESSAYS

Contents

List of exercises

Introduction
Crystal power

People say that stones do not speak,
they do not feel. What an error!
ALPHONSE DE CHATEAUBRIANT, *LA RÉPONSE DU SEIGNEUR*

Think of crystals... What comes to mind? The universally accepted definition of a crystal is 'a solid body with a geometrically regular shape'. It includes not only sparkling gemstones but also semi-precious stones and even rocks. The crystals we are meeting in this book are, for the most part, the crystalline form of minerals. They include precious and semi-precious stones and also some rocks. These gifts from the Earth offer healing, wisdom and so much more.

Crystals have been used for an extremely long time. It might surprise you to know that they were universally regarded as sacred in the ancient world and were an integral part of religious, medicinal, protective and divinatory practices. In India, Shiva Lingams, stone representations of the god Shiva, are worshipped to this day, while according to researcher Robert Temple, 'The ancient Greek Pythagoreans of the fifth century BCE believed that the sun was a gigantic crystal ball larger than the Earth, which gathered the ambient light of the surrounding cosmos and refracted it to Earth, acting as a giant lens.' Other early civilizations believed that the cosmos was a series of nested crystal spheres.

Crystals do underpin our planet. They are the Earth's bones and its fundamental geometry. They carry the planet's subtle energy in much the same way that nerves and blood vessels carry electrochemical messages around the physical body. But they also power our world. Found in the latest technology and medical equipment, and even the paint on our walls, they are an indispensable part of modern life. If you wear jewellery or a watch, you are already bathed in crystal-generated energy. Computers would not function were it not for the piezoelectric properties of Quartz. The crystals themselves form their own crystalline internet. The push to find new mineral riches has always been behind the exploration of the terrestrial world, and now it fuels the flight to the stars. But the use of crystals is as old as humanity itself.

Sensual magic

Crystals are a sensual and intuitive experience rather than an intellectual pursuit. They have a unique ability to absorb and transmute negativity into beneficence – and to interact with us energetically. Their ability to harness the power of our mind is truly incredible – they amp up the energy, boosting whatever we do. And it's through handling them that we really connect to their magic.

If you've never worked with crystals before, you're in for a treat. These scrumptious beings pack a potent punch and you'll be amazed at the ways in which they enhance your life. Not merely decorative, they are protective and life-affirming too. They can increase your energy, enhance your wellbeing, help you to keep calm in a crisis, change the way you think, ensure your space is safe, offer you guidance and much else besides.

To begin with, just pick up a Quartz crystal. Hold it lightly in your hand for a minute or two. Do you feel a tingling vibration or a pulsing in your hand? If so, you're experiencing the energy of the crystal. (If you feel nothing, try changing hands.)

Using this book

This book has been carefully structured to take you through working with crystals a step at a time. Practical exercises and case histories are included to expand your sensitivity to crystal energy and its potential, and portraits of individual crystals are given to introduce you to the crystals used in the exercises. There's also a glossary at the end to explain any terms you haven't come across before and a resource directory to guide you to further exploration. All you need is an open mind and the willingness to experiment.

Please don't skip the preparatory chapters. A little time spent in Part I will repay you with the most potent crystal energies. The essential foundation, it introduces the information you need to use your crystals to best effect. There are important stages to go through before you can fully appreciate crystal power. You need to open your palm chakras so that you *feel* crystal energy, for instance, and to attune to your crystals before using them so that you *sense* their energy.

When you move on to Part II, the practical applications, you can fruitfully spend several days on each exercise, trying out various crystals. Or you can simply skim through to find what interests you or is of particular relevance to you at that moment. But again, this section is structured to help you make the most of your experience. Your personal energies need to be high and your space clear and safe before you expand your awareness, for example. Also in Part II, you'll meet the mysterious crystal skulls and the crystal mentors who can offer guidance on your path through life.

Skill-building

You'll find plenty here to excite you. By exploring different applications of crystal power, you'll also form your crystal knowledge into a useful toolkit and build skills that can be applied in a variety of situations. By the time you've finished, you'll have tasted a wide spectrum of crystal possibilities and be aware of how to find more in-depth information and explore further.

Take your time

It's exciting to find a new crystal or a fresh skill and you may want to rush ahead. But practice really does make perfect. The more you practise an exercise, the more it becomes part of your skill set and the more your crystals communicate with you. So, as you go through this book, write down your response to a crystal or an exercise, then repeat it and compare your results. Note how your ability to sense energy expands each time you interact with your crystals.

Crystal encapsulation

As well as including old favourites, this book introduces some of the newer and rarer crystals, which can be expensive. If you don't have access to these crystals, you can use my *Crystal Wisdom Oracle* cards instead, as the photographs beautifully encapsulate the energy of the crystals. This is an excellent way to try a crystal before you buy it – and you can use the cards as a guide through life.

The way forward

There is no one right way to work with crystals, only the way that is right for you. Just as a crystal has its own unique vibration, each person has their own unique energetic frequency, which will respond more strongly to some crystals than others. And everyone attunes to crystals in their own way. By the time you've worked through this book, you'll have discovered that for yourself. Be flexible and you'll soon find the way forward.

Part I
CRYSTAL FOUNDATIONS

In the following chapters you'll learn what crystals are, what they can do for you and how to care for them.

Chapter 1
First find your crystals

et's start our exploration by taking a brief look at the structure of crystals. A crystal is basically a package of energy and minerals in an orderly three-dimensional lattice. Each type of crystal has a unique geometric pattern, with symmetrically arranged plane-faces and a specific chemical composition.

Although crystals might look solid, like everything else in the universe they are actually a few particles vibrating in a great deal of seemingly empty space. The ancients, and most crystal workers today, would argue that this space is filled with divine energy or consciousness, and we'll be exploring this idea later. For now, let's look at how modern crystal practitioners understand crystals:

'Crystals remind us of the structures upon which our universe is built. All matter, everything that is physical and solid, owes its existence to the organizing properties of crystals.'

SUE AND SIMON LILLY, *HEALING WITH CRYSTALS AND CHAKRA ENERGIES*

'Stones emit radiation and, being extremely durable and very permanent... they emit the same information in a very constant way. They could be compared to radio transmitters that constantly broadcast the same programme. Every stone or crystal has its own specific light, or to put it another way, its specific radiation that naturally influences our organisms. If contact is made between a crystal and our bodies, the absorbed light will inevitably be an influence on the 'light concentration' between the cells and cause certain reactions.'

MICHAEL GIENGER, *CRYSTAL POWER, CRYSTAL HEALING*

'Are stones alive? Of course we know that, in terms of biology's definition of life, they are not. Yet crystals grow, they sometimes decay, and, perhaps most importantly, they seem to communicate with us.'

ROBERT SIMMONS, *THE BOOK OF STONES*

Robert Simmons gives us a glimpse of the mysteries to come. He is reiterating a very old belief that crystals are living beings.

To get the most out of crystals, you need to find those that are truly *yours*. Each person has a unique energy frequency and the secret to effective crystal working is to find the crystals that respond to you.

Which is the crystal for you?

Everyone who is interested in crystals has had the experience of a crystal 'winking' at them. You go into a shop or trawl the internet and a crystal catches your eye. This is the one for you. It is not necessarily the biggest, prettiest or priciest. It may be a raw lump, tumbled or faceted. But it is the most potent for you personally.

So, go into a shop and see what calls to you. These eager beings have been longing to work with you. Now is the time. You can also use my *Crystal Wisdom Oracle* cards, which allow you to feel the energies from a photograph, or the photographs in *101 Power Crystals*, or look at the pictures on www.angeladditions.co.uk or any of the other crystal suppliers in the Resources section and see which crystals call to you. You can also dowse (*see page 17*), or look at what you already have in your collection. But whatever you do, first open the chakras in your palms and set your root in place.

The palm chakras

There is one simple thing that enables the maximum contact with crystals, and that is opening the energy-sensitive chakras in the centre of your palms. Although these chakras are little known, they are what make healing and *feeling* crystal energies so potent.

Exercise: Opening the palm chakras

✦ Open and close your hands, forming fists, several times.

✦ Bring your hands together with straight fingers so that the palms touch.

✦ Flex your fingers down and open your hands slightly, then bring them back together again.

- Repeat several times. Your palms may start to tingle and it will feel as though a ball of energy is building up between them. This indicates that your palm chakras are opening.

- Always open these chakras before choosing or working with a crystal.

Growing your root (shamanic anchor)

The second thing that makes working with crystal energies easier – and helps you to feel secure – is to open the Earth Star chakra, or energy centre, beneath your feet. This chakra helps you to grow a 'root' that goes deep down into the Earth and grounds your energies. Earth energy travels up this root and healing energy goes down through it, setting up a circuit that helps you channel subtle crystal energy into the physical dimension and makes your crystal work more power-full.

Exercise: Opening the Earth Star chakra

- Stand for a few moments with your feet slightly apart, your knees relaxed and somewhat bent and your hands loosely clasped beneath your navel over your sacral chakra (see page 102).

- Picture a dinner-plate-sized vortex of energy spinning beneath your feet.

- Consciously make a connection through your hands, across to your hips, down each leg and out through your feet to the vortex below.

- Picture the Earth Star vortex opening like a flower to receive the two strands of energy.

- As you make the connection, bounce a little to strengthen it.

✦ Visualize the energy cords twining together to make a root that goes deep down into the Earth and anchors itself to the huge iron crystal at the core. This cord is your shamanic anchor. It holds you lightly on the Earth.

✦ Open the Earth Star chakra whenever you work with crystal energies.

What do you want your crystal to do?

One way to start out is to think about what you want your crystal to do for you. Do you want it to enhance your environment? Heal you? Show you the future? These are some of the things you might want from your crystal:

✦ 'To help me to feel safe.'

✦ 'To make me feel good.'

✦ 'To protect me from electromagnetic emanations.'

✦ 'To protect me from geopathic stress.'

If any of the above statements describes what you want your crystal to do, read Part I and then go to Chapter 13 to learn about personal protection and find recommended crystals.

✦ 'To look pretty.'

✦ 'To decorate my room.'

✦ 'To make me and my space feel good.'

If the above statements apply to you, read Part I and then go to chapters 14 and 15 to learn about space clearing and environmental enhancement.

❖   'To help me relax.'

❖   'To switch off my mind.'

If the above apply to you, read Part I and then go to Chapter 16.

❖   'To change how I think and feel.'

❖   'To enable me to meditate more deeply.'

❖   'To help me journey into other worlds or dimensions.'

❖   'To connect to my guardian angels or crystal mentor.'

If any of the above statements describes what you want your crystal to do, read Part I and then go to chapters 12 and 19.

❖   'To give me guidance.'

❖   'To enable me to explore my options.'

❖   'To help me make decisions.'

❖   'To allow me to contemplate my future.'

If the above apply to you, read Part I and then go to chapters 17, 19 and 20.

❖   'To help me connect to the mysterious power of crystals.'

❖   'To show me how to talk to the crystal oversouls.'

❖   'To allow me to discover more about the magical history of crystals.'

If the above statements apply to you, read Part I and then go to chapters 12, 13, 16, 17, 19 and 20 to explore the legendary properties of crystals and how they can help you to foresee the future, and connect to the mysterious crystal skulls that are said to communicate with humankind.

Letting a crystal find you

Now you've identified what you want your crystal to do, try the following exercises to help you choose the right crystal.

Exercise: Exercising your intuition

❖ Walk into a crystal shop and let yourself be pulled in a particular direction rather than thinking about where to go.

❖ See which crystal catches your eye. You will need to take it home and purify it (*see page 22*) before working with it, as crystals pick up the energy of everyone who has handled them.

If you have a crystal collection already, you have exercised your intuition in picking them – or they have selected you. You can exercise your intuition further by choosing which crystal to work with now.

❖ Simply look at your collection with softly focused eyes and see which crystal winks at you.

❖ Alternatively, open your palm chakras and let your fingers intuitively pick a crystal up. Hold it gently to connect to its energies. (*It may need purifying and activating, in which case move on to Chapter 2.*)

Exercise: The power of touch

❖ Open your palm chakras.

❖ If you already have a selection of crystals, place them on a table. If you are in a shop, stand by the crystal display.

◆ Close your eyes and, if working with your own crystals and they aren't too delicate, gently move them around.

◆ With your eyes still closed, move your hand over the crystals in a circular motion until one pulls your hand towards it or you feel a tingle in your palm. If nothing happens, try your other hand or purify your crystals (*see page 22*) and then try again.

◆ If you're in a shop and nothing immediately jumps out at you, open your palm chakras and run your fingers through the tubs of crystals. One will stick to your fingers or feel particularly good. This is your crystal.

◆ If you find you can't put a crystal down, that's the one for you.

◆ Keep a note of the crystals that choose you and your immediate insights into how they want to work with you. Other insights will develop later. Write those down too.

Exercise: Choosing in the comfort of your home

The internet is a great tool for crystal selection from the comfort of your home – once your sensitivity is turned on.

◆ Log on to one of the sites in the Resources section (*see page 239*) or to your favourite crystal site, preferably one that shows you several photographs of the same type of crystal.

◆ Look at the screen with half-closed eyes and run through the pictures until one catches your eye.

◆ Once a crystal has called to you, purchase it.

Exercise: Let your eyes do the choosing

❖ If you have crystal books such as *101 Power Crystals* or the *Crystal Wisdom Oracle* card pack (*see Resources*), flick through the pictures or let the pages fall open at a particular entry or let a card call to you out of the pack. The illustrations in my *101 Power Crystals* and *Crystal Wisdom Oracle* are particularly useful for this, as the remarkable photographs really capture the energy of the crystals, as do those posted on www.angeladditions.co.uk which were taken by my daughter, Jeni Campbell, of crystals that have been specially attuned by me.

❖ While your eyes are softly focused, ask the crystal to connect more strongly with you so that you sense its energy. Let it speak to you (*see chapters 2 and 19*).

❖ When you have found your crystal, buy it!

Dowsing

Dowsing is an excellent way to choose crystals. There are two methods, one using a pendulum and the other using your fingers.

Exercise: Finding your pendulum

Pendulums are crafted from a variety of crystals or woods in different sizes and weights. Choose one that interacts well with your energy to make dowsing more productive. Good crystal shops never mind if you try out several before buying.

❖ Put a variety of pendulums on the table in front of you.

❖ Open your palm chakras (*see page 11*).

❖ Let your eyes go loosely out of focus and move from pendulum to pendulum.

❖ When one particularly catches your eye, pick it up and hold it.

❖ Sense how it feels in your hand. Take a moment to attune to it.

❖ Try dowsing with it (*see below*).

❖ You may like to compare and contrast several pendulums before making your final selection.

Using your pendulum

To use a pendulum you need to establish your 'yes', 'no' and 'maybe'. Once you know your 'yes' and 'no' indications, hold the pendulum over a crystal and ask, 'Is this the right crystal for me?' If the answer is a rather half-hearted 'yes' or 'maybe', ask, 'Is there a better one?' If the answer is 'yes', check out whether it's another crystal of the same type or whether a different type would be better.

Exercise: Pendulum dowsing – establishing 'yes' and 'no'

❖ The easiest method is to hold the pendulum loosely with the chain wrapped around your fingers and anchored lightly with your thumb. Leave about a hand's breadth of chain hanging down. Experiment with what works best for you. Some people simply hold a pendulum between their thumb and forefinger.

❖ Hold the pendulum over your knee and ask, 'Is my name [give your real name]?' The pendulum will move of its own volition, either circling or swinging from side to side. Note which way it circles or swings, as this is your 'yes' answer.

❖ Then ask the same question but give a false name. This gives your 'no' answer – the pendulum will circle or swing in another direction.

❖ If you mix your first name with a false surname, you will get a 'don't know/maybe' – which is often a kind of shimmy of the pendulum without much movement.

Finger dowsing

Finger dowsing is a quick and easy alternative to pendulum dowsing. It gives you an instant, strong 'yes' or 'no' answer.

Exercise: Finger dowsing

❖ To finger dowse, simply press the forefinger and thumb of one hand together in a loop.

❖ Through the loop, link the forefinger and thumb of the other hand.

❖ As you ask your question, pull gently. If the answer is 'yes', the loop will hold. If 'no', your hands will pull apart easily.

How many crystals do I need?

Each crystal has its own unique vibration – its frequency or wavelength. These frequencies range from earthy to extremely high, and some crystals combine both, grounding the energies. A high-vibration crystal isn't better than an earthy one, it's simply different. Each type of crystal has a specific task to do.

Finding the appropriate vibration for the work you need a crystal to do helps the crystal to work at optimum efficiency. So, a crystal toolkit of about seven or eight basic crystals with an additional few high-vibration ones will be just right. You might like to purchase *The Crystal Healing Pack*, which has crystals for each of the chakras (*see Chapter 9*), and add one or two high-vibration stones of your choice.

SUMMARY

❖ A crystal is a package of energy and minerals in an orderly three-dimensional lattice.

❖ Each type of crystal has a unique geometric pattern.

❖ Each person has a unique energy frequency. To get the most out of crystals you need to find ones that resonate with your energy field.

❖ The best way to choose a crystal is with your intuition or by dowsing.

❖ Look at what you already have in your collection.

❖ First open the chakras in your palms and set your root in place.

Chapter 2
Preparing your crystals

To fully harness the power of your crystals, you need to take a few essential steps first. As crystals rapidly absorb negative energies and pick up the vibes of everyone who handles them, they need to be kept purified, so they require cleansing both before and after use.

They also need to be activated so that they work to their fullest potential. People often say, 'Crystals don't work for me,' and when I reply, 'Have you asked them to?' they are surprised. But asking your crystals to work with you for your highest good – and that of others – amps up their power enormously.

You also need to look at what you intend to do with your crystal. Intention is the power that focuses your crystal on the task ahead. When you hold an intention, it directs the crystal energy. It's a bit like putting the correct program onto your computer – you wouldn't expect it to work without – but a crystal has its own intelligence and may well do even more than you asked.

So, let's look at these essential steps now.

Remember, always work in an energetically clear, safe space (*see Chapter 14*).

First cleanse your crystal

This is a fundamental rule of working with crystals. No matter whether you're working with a favourite crystal you've had for a long time or one you've just bought home from a shop, a crystal needs cleansing before use.

And it needs cleansing after use too. People say, 'This crystal used to work, but now it's stopped.' When asked, 'Have you cleaned it?', they look perplexed. To keep a crystal working at optimum level, it needs regular cleansing and re-energizing. This is especially the case with crystal jewellery, which will be working for you whether you intend it to or not, so you may as well help it along. It will be collecting energies and will transmute them and pass on its properties to you as long as it's kept clean.

Also note that crystals that are on display need to be cleansed frequently.

Exercise: Cleansing a crystal

✦ If your crystal is tumbled or robust, hold it under running water for a few minutes or carefully immerse it in a stream or the sea. Remember that salt water damages delicate crystals, especially those with many points on a bed or layers, so use it with care. Alternatively, use a drop of a proprietary crystal cleanser or spray your crystal with it. (To make a spray bottle, put 7 drops of the essence into pure spring water. You can add essential oils or vodka as a preservative, but the spray will keep for several days without. *See Resources.*)

❖ If the crystal is delicate, layered or friable, place it in brown rice overnight or pass it through the light of a candle or the smoke from a smudge stick, or use a proprietary cleanser in a spray bottle.

❖ Pop the crystal into sunlight or moonlight to recharge its batteries, or use a proprietary crystal recharger. One drop or a quick spray and it's done.

Exercise: Feeling the difference

❖ Hold an uncleansed crystal for a few moments and note what you feel. Pay attention to your whole body as well as your hands.

❖ Then cleanse the crystal and hold it again and note the changes.

Asking a crystal to work with you

Crystals are very wise beings who see much further than we do, but if you don't ask one to work with you, how does it know what you want it to do? Having said that, I try not to be too specific, as I feel it restricts the crystal if I only ask from my limited Earth perspective. So I ask for the crystal to work for my highest good and that of other people, and to do what is appropriate for my personal and spiritual growth, and I add 'this or something better' or 'as appropriate' to requests. There are times when I feel stuck in a situation I'd much rather get out of, but if there's something I need to learn from it, or a gift I need to gain, scrambling out too quickly may lose me that opportunity. Therefore, I would rather have a crystal support me as I go *through* the necessary challenge and out the other side.

Exercise: Programming and charging

Holding a crystal and focusing on it for a few moments charges it up, filling it with intention.

❖ If you have a specific purpose in mind for your crystal, hold it between your hands.

❖ Concentrate your thoughts on the crystal and ask it to cooperate with you to fulfil that purpose in the best way possible and to attune itself to your purpose.

❖ Once you have stated your intention, let it go. To go on focusing on it is to force the energy, and that is counterproductive.

Getting to know your crystals

Each time you become the keeper of a new crystal, take the time to attune to it.

Exercise: Attuning to a crystal

❖ Open your palm chakras (*see page 11*) and sit quietly holding your crystal in your hands.

❖ Breathe gently and focus your attention on the crystal. Ask that it works with you in love and truth for your highest good.

❖ Half close your eyes and simply gaze at your crystal. Ask it to communicate with you in the most appropriate way for you.

❖ Continue to breathe gently and be receptive to the response you get – which may come in the form of a bodily sensation, a feeling or an intuition.

✦ After a few minutes, notice how you feel. Are you calm and relaxed, or twitchy and jittery? Is an emotion rising? Does a particular part of your body tingle or ache? Is one of your chakras lighting up? (*You'll find a chakra diagram on page 94 if you are unfamiliar with the location of these.*)

✦ Move your crystal around your body to check out sensations and intuitions. If it feels good to keep it in a particular place, leave it there for a while. Don't force anything, simply allow things to happen. Let the crystal be your guide.

✦ Ask yourself if your crystal is dropping thoughts into your mind. If so, trust the process. Or has your crystal found another way to communicate, through bodily or intuitive sensation, and so on? Crystals are creative beings.

✦ After five minutes or so, thank the crystal for its work, put it to one side and consciously disconnect your attention from it, unless your intuition tells you to keep it in your pocket or somewhere close by.

✦ Repeat for your other crystals.

Case history: Connecting to universal love

I picked up a piece of Tugtupite and held it to my heart. Instantly I felt my heart expand until it filled the whole universe. I was connected to everything and felt universal love flowing into and through every part of my being and into my cells – which included all the other parts of the universe. Everything was love. Even when I put the crystal down, the love stayed with me and I felt deep compassion for everything. (Source: workshop participant.)

If a crystal doesn't feel right

If you don't respond to the crystal within a few moments, put it aside and ask yourself, 'Have I cleansed this crystal?' Then ask yourself, 'Have I asked it to work with me?' Pick it up again, follow the steps above and if you still don't feel in harmony with it, put it aside for now. Not every person responds to a specific crystal, or responds in the same way, even when they are in harmony with it.

Also, not every crystal will suit you, as your individual energy patterns will harmonize better with some crystal frequencies than others. It may be that a crystal that causes you discomfort when attuning simply isn't the crystal for you at this time, so try another type. If a crystal feels uncomfortable or unappealing, however, it might be stirring up issues that need addressing later. If this is the case, see my book *Life-Changing Crystals*. That's why learning to attune to a crystal quickly helps you to select exactly the right crystal for you, rather than picking one that someone else suggests. When you are starting out, always work with crystals that feel good.

Recording your experience

To get the most from your attunement sessions with crystals, write down all that you remember from them in a notebook. Record:

1.   The date and time.

2.   The moon phase (dark, new, waxing, waning or full).

3.   Your mood before you started.

4.   The type of crystal.

5. What you experienced.

6. How you felt afterwards.

This helps keep track of the effect that different crystals have on you, but it also charts whether you are more sensitive to crystal energies at particular times – the moon cycle affects your sensitivity, for instance, as can the time of day.

Deprogramming a crystal

Once you no longer need a crystal, deprogram it and put it away for a rest. People often forget to do this. Although cleansing may sometimes be sufficient, specific programs do need careful and intentional dismantling.

Exercise: Deprogramming

✦   To deprogram a crystal, cleanse it, then hold it in your hands.

✦   Thank it for working on your behalf and state that the work is now complete. Ask that any program in the crystal is dissolved and the crystal becomes quiescent until required again.

✦   You may wish to state that if the crystal is working on your behalf at a higher level of which you are unaware, it continues with that work.

Keeping your crystals active

Crystals benefit from regular cleansing and recharging. Having a monthly 'crystal day' when you purify your crystals and then put them out into the sunlight or moonlight to recharge helps you to attune more closely with them and raises your own energies too. You can also meditate with your crystals then to see if they have anything to share with you (*see Chapter 16*).

Storing your crystals

Keep your crystal(s) in a drawer or box when not in use. Tumbled crystals can be stored together in a bag – add a Carnelian to keep them energetically purified and cleansed – but delicate crystals need to be wrapped separately.

SUMMARY ✐

❖ Crystals need cleansing and programming before and after use.

❖ Always ask your crystal to work with you.

❖ Intention is the power that focuses your crystal on the task ahead.

❖ If a crystal doesn't feel right for you, it may be because it is pushing your buttons. To begin with, work with crystals that feel good.

Chapter 3
'A heap of blessings numerous as the sands'

Crystals have been used for protection, divination and healing in every region of the world for at least 7,000 years. In the ancient world, rocks weren't just chosen for their beauty as adornments or their strength as building materials; their innate abilities to carry electromagnetic and other Earth currents were also utilized. Rocks containing a high proportion of piezoelectric Quartz were the material of choice for stone circles, temples and tombs right across the ancient world. Quartz kerbstones may have protected the dead – and enabled the spirits of the ancestors to communicate with the living.

Theophrastus on Stones, the earliest known Greek scientific treatise, deals expressly with the properties of minerals and the products derived from them. Dating to the fourth century BCE, it was the source for the Roman geographer Pliny's commentary on stones in his *Natural History* and, most probably, for the unknown author of the *Lithica*, a fourth-century lapidary, which tells us that crystals are 'a sure remede against each earthly woe'. The book recounts the numerous ways in which amulets, precious and semi-precious stones were used:

Enjoying [crystal] wealth, in its possession sure,
No care, no sorrow shall he ever taste.
Nor pining sickness his strong body waste...
Nor, dreading his foes' might, from battle flee,
Abandoning the hope of victory...

In regal courts he honour shall command...
And the soft maid, by love's strong impulse led,
Shall gently draw towards the golden bed.
His prayers shall ever reach the Immortals' ear,
Angry seas nor tempests shall he fear...
Him, though alone, shall savage robbers flee...
He shall at will the hidden thoughts perceive,
Which others in their inmost hearts conceive.
And what the birds, the inmates of the sky,
Those winged interpreters of heaven's decrees...
He learns the dragon's rushing force to break,
And quench the venom of the crawling snake...
The man dashed to the ground in that dire hour
When reels his brain 'neath Luna's baleful power,
I'll teach his cure, and how the pest to tame...
And how to ban by spells the dead man's ghost...

This extract describes healing, protection, divine intervention, attracting abundance and love, honing psychic abilities, banishing unquiet spirits and taming natural forces – all applications of crystal power today.

Amulets for protection from harm

Few people in the ancient world would have dreamed of undertaking a venture without an amulet – an object worn or carried to protect them from harm. Crystals were often used for this purpose. Small children were given protective strings of Bloodstone, Carnelian and Jasper to ensure their wellbeing from birth. Priests used the stones for healing and for protection against the evils of the everyday and supernatural worlds. A bishop's Amethyst ring today carries the same power of protection and blessing.

Exercise: Making an amulet

❖ Choose an appropriate cleansed (*see page 22*), tumbled or shaped crystal. If you wish to wear your amulet, choose one with a hole.

❖ Open your palm chakras (*see page 11*).

❖ Hold the stone in your hands for a few moments and ask it to give you protection, good health, abundance or whatever your purpose is. Be clear and specific about what you wish the stone to do.

❖ If you work with a personal deity or angelic being, ask that it imbues the stone with its presence.

❖ If you work with symbols, draw the appropriate symbol on the stone with an indelible marker pen.

❖ Place the stone in a pouch and put it in your pocket or around your neck, or thread the amulet onto a cord and wear it constantly.

Traditional amulet stones include Agate, Amethyst, Bloodstone, Carnelian, Chrysoprase, Emerald, Flint, Jade, Jasper, Sardonyx, Smoky Quartz and Tiger's Eye.

Crystal portrait: Carnelian

Vibration: Earthy

A powerfully energizing crystal. The protection and good fortune amulet stone. Inspires success in business, brings abundance. Grounds and anchors you in your present surroundings. Protects against rage and resentment. Increases fertility and creativity. Continually charges up your energy.

Keep one in your car to protect against road rage. Place one inside your front door to draw in abundance.

Crystal shamanism

The use of crystals goes back a long way. Eight and a half thousand years ago a young shaman was laid to rest on a bed of red Haematite at Bad Dürrenberg, her magical grave goods beside her. They included numerous bones, 31 tiny Flint blades in a crane's bone box and a carefully fashioned stone ball that could be rolled rather like dice.

Five thousand years ago in Mesopotamia, a woman was interred with 12 pebbles beside her, her only grave goods. They were collected from 200 miles away. It is tempting to think, along with the professor who uncovered the grave, that they had a specific purpose: divination. Early Mesopotamian sources describe an *elmeshu* (probably clear Quartz) that functioned as an oracle stone.

In the Old Testament the breastplate of the high priest was not only studded with flashing crystals, it also carried the Urim and Thummin, oracular items that ascertained the will of God and the future of the Jewish nation. These are believed to have been meteorites, which were highly sacred throughout the ancient world (*see Chapter 18*).

Crystal healing

Crystals were also part of early medical practice and this continued into more modern times. Crystals listed in the medical papyri of ancient Egypt formed an important part of treatment right up to the eighteenth century. The tradition passed into the magical and medical lexicons of East and West, and crystals are the basis for many modern pharmaceuticals. Minerals such as lithium, found in Kunzite and other depression-alleviating crystals, are still used in conventional medicine today.

Modern usage

Quite simply, the modern world couldn't function without crystals. They are found throughout industry, generating and storing energy. Rare-earth minerals are highly prized in the innovative-technology field. Diamond bits are effective cutting tools. Kyanite is found in spark plugs. Medical lasers are focused through Rubies. Quartz powers ultrasound. Computers run on silicon chips – thin slivers of Quartz. Russian naval boats are being coated with anti-radar paint created from reflective fullerene-based Shungite, a mineral used in crystal healing for protection and wellbeing. Many modern crystals are manufactured, but have their base in the natural crystal world.

Crystal portrait: Shungite

Vibration: Earthy and high

Shungite contains virtually all the minerals in the periodic table. A rare carbon mineral, it is composed of fullerenes – 'Buckyballs' (spherical) or 'Buckytubes' (cylindrical). It is found only in Karelia, northern Russia, and is at least 2 billion years old. It was laid down before organic life was established, and yet carbon-based minerals normally arise from decayed organic matter, so it has been suggested that an enormous meteorite hit the Earth and created the crater in which Lake Onega and the Shungite formed. Although the lake is highly polluted, the water flowing from it is purified by the Shungite and has been used for healing for hundreds of years.

Research has shown that Shungite is antiviral and antibacterial. It absorbs whatever is hazardous to health, whether that be pesticides, free radicals, bacteria and the like, or EMF, microwave and other vibrational emissions. It transforms water into a biologically active life-enhancing substance, whilst at the same time removing harmful micro-organisms and pollutants (*see page 243*). It boosts physical wellbeing and has a powerful effect on the immune system. Restoring emotional equilibrium, it transmutes stress into a potent energetic recharge. Wear Shungite or place it on the source of EMF emissions such as computers and cell phones to eliminate their detrimental effect on sensitive human energy systems.

Petaltone EMF Protection essence works particularly well when placed on Shungite.

Note: As Shungite is a rapid absorber of negative energy and pollutants, it needs to be cleansed frequently.

SUMMARY ✍

- The use of crystals for protection, divination and healing goes back at least 7,000 years.

- Crystals were used throughout every region of the world.

- Crystals formed part of early medical practice and continued to do so into more modern times.

- They were always popular for protective amulets.

- Crystals have many modern applications.

Chapter 4
'A casket of jewels fair'

Understanding how crystals were formed, the secret ingredients that went into their alchemical creation and the universal geometry that underlies their construction throws light on the way energy flows through them. Each crystal belongs to an overall chemical 'family', such as sulphides or carbonates, which 'speaks' in a different way. Once you comprehend a crystal's language, you know how its energy functions.

Where do crystals come from?

Rocks, and the crystals within them, are created out of minerals by a variety of processes, mostly from the molten rock, magma, at the core of the planet. Most are crystallized minerals. Some solidified from gases and interstellar dust during the primary formation of Earth or were pressured and baked into existence. Others exploded out of volcanoes or dripped into being. Some were compressed and metamorphosed as the planet itself transformed. Others were ground up and redeposited in layers. A few formed so fast they lack internal crystalline structure. One or two arrived from outer space.

Crystal formation

Primary: The most ancient rocks on the planet, primary crystals formed deep under the Earth's crust from the seed material of the universe. Liquefied or gaseous minerals cooled and crystallized, or exploded up the vents of an active volcano. If the magma cooled slowly, it created large crystals. If it cooled quickly, it formed small crystals. Material that cooled rapidly created non-crystalline Obsidian glass.

Holding raw primal power, primary crystals stimulate growth processes. They impel change, restore stability and ground energies, helping to heal the past.

Secondary: Sedimentary crystals are ones reformed from primary material. Erosion wears rock down to tiny particles which are then deposited and cemented together again, often underwater. Dead marine creatures too create depositional rocks.

Sedimentary rocks allow energy to move freely. They resonate with the cycles of death, decay and rebirth.

Tertiary: Deep underground, hot rock is subjected to enormous pressure and/or chemical change, which modifies its structure. Tertiary crystals are created as mountain ranges collide, or primary rocks are superheated and metamorphosis occurs.

These metamorphic crystals facilitate change and transmutation.

Tektites: Meteorites from outer space collide with our planet. Many are metallic-looking, polished and worn to a fraction of their size by friction as they pass through the Earth's atmosphere. Occasionally a bigger meteorite makes it through, only to fragment on impact and fuse with the Earth, creating Moldavite or Libyan Glass.

Tektites help us to gain an overview, uniting cosmic wisdom and earthly sensibilities.

What are crystals made from?

The base material of crystals is either a single mineral alone, which is rare, or several minerals in combination. These are organized into internationally recognized crystallochemical classifications:

- Carbonates. *Examples:* Azurite, Calcite

- Halides. *Examples:* Fluorite, Halite

- Native elements (unadulterated and uncombined). *Examples:* Diamond, Gold

- Oxides. *Examples:* Chrysoberyl, Sapphire

- Phosphates and Arsenates. *Examples:* Apatite, Turquoise

- Silicates (subdivided into further groups). *Examples:* Danburite, Quartz

- Sulphates. *Examples:* Celestine, Desert Rose

- Sulphides and sulphosalts. *Examples:* Bornite, Cinnabar

These mineral families each provide a unique chemical base, then tiny alterations and adulterations produce a unique crystal. Take silicate dioxide, for instance. Quartz is basically a silicate dioxide. It has large or small crystals depending on how quickly it cooled. Chalcedony, another form of silicate dioxide, cooled rapidly inside small pockets. It has tiny crystals, although Carnelian, a form of Chalcedony, can be a much larger mass. Flint, laid down from the bodies of sea creatures, is non-crystalline pure silica. Amethyst, Citrine, Rose and Smoky Quartzes are all subtle variations of silicate dioxide combined with other minerals to produce their individual colour (*see below*).

Saved from the crusher

A question that perplexes many people is whether or not crystals should be removed from the Earth. Mining is big business these days and few small ethical mining operations are left. I try to buy my crystals from ethical sources, but it's not always possible. So I asked my crystal mentors (*see page 221*) about this. The answer was that they appreciated the work that crystal healers were doing, as this counteracted the wholesale ravishing of the Earth. They told me that certain crystals willingly offered themselves up to assist with Earth healing and other tasks. They looked on it as fulfilling their purpose – literally what they were made for. Lemurian Seed Crystals have said that they were carefully placed and covered up by crystal workers aeons ago so that they could perform their function now. Other crystals were greatly relieved when they were saved from the crusher. Although one mentor did point out that even when a crystal had been crushed to become an ingredient in paint, medicine or technology, it could still radiate its energy.

SUMMARY ✎

❖ Crystals, and the rocks that contain them, are formed out of minerals by primary, secondary and tertiary processes.

❖ How crystals are formed, the secret ingredients that go into their alchemical creation and the universal geometry that underlies their construction throw light on the way energy flows through them.

❖ Each crystal belongs to an overall chemical 'family' which 'speaks' in a different way.

❖ Once you comprehend a crystal's language, you know how its energy functions.

Chapter 5
Nature's building blocks

Some crystals are shining, glamorous – and expensive. Others are rough, seemingly dull. Many crystals are tumbled, cut or faceted to enhance their appearance, but work just as well in their natural form, although the external shape does alter how the crystal energy is experienced. All crystals generate, store, regulate, transmit and absorb energy, but the fundamental energy-focusing tool is shape.

Universal building blocks

As the ancient Greek mathematician Pythagoras (whose father was a gem-cutter) noted, the universe is made up of a mere handful of geometric shapes. Crystals reflect these universal building blocks.

Atoms form the heart of a crystal. Inside an atom, dynamic particles rotate in constant motion around a central point, generating energy. So, although a crystal may look outwardly serene, it is actually a seething molecular mass vibrating at a specific, but variable, frequency.

Individual crystals are recognizable by how their component molecules stick together to fill space. Chemical impurities, radiation, Earth-energy and solar emissions, and the way they form, mean that each type of crystal has its own unique signature or crystal lattice. Under a microscope, a large or small version, or different colour, of the same crystal has exactly the same lattice. It is this structure that is crucial to crystal classification. Several types of crystals may form from the same mineral, or combination of minerals, but each type has crystallized differently. However, crystals that have an outwardly different appearance may be classified as the same type. For example, to the naked eye the brown 'sputnik' form of Aragonite has no outward connection with its pale pink, layered, blue or spiky white relations, but they are classified as the same crystal because their component minerals and internal crystal lattice match exactly.

Geometric forms

Crystals are built from one of seven geometric forms, plus a non-geometric anomaly, that lock together into a number of potential crystal shapes. These crystal systems have generic names based on their internal geometry. Each functions in a slightly different way, channelling energy according to its crystal lattice.

❖ **Amorphous:** Lacking an inner structure, amorphous crystals allow energy to pass through freely, act rapidly and may be a catalyst for growth. *Example:* Obsidian

❖ **Hexagonal:** Highly energetic hexagonal crystals are particularly useful for energy balancing and for exploring specific issues. *Example:* Rhodochrosite

✦ **Isometric (Cubic):** Stabilizing and grounding, cubic crystals are excellent for structure and reorganization. This is the only crystal form that does not bend light rays as they pass through it. *Example:* Fluorite

✦ **Monoclinic:** Purifying monoclinic crystals enhance perception. *Example*: Azurite

✦ **Orthorhombic:** Vibrantly energetic, orthorhombic crystals are useful cleansers and clearers. *Example:* Peridot

✦ **Tetragonal:** Absorbing and transforming energy, tetragonals are excellent balancers and resolvers. *Example:* Idocrase

✦ **Triclinic:** Integrating energy and opposites, triclinic crystals assist in exploring other dimensions. *Example*: Astrophyllite

✦ **Trigonal:** Creating and radiating energy, trigonals are invigorating and protective, rebalancing the aura. *Example:* All types of Quartz

Crystal practitioner Michael Gienger identified a series of lifestyles built around these fundamental crystal systems and created an intuitive crystal healing method based upon them. You'll find more details in his *Crystal Power, Crystal Healing* (*see Resources*).

The effect of external shape

Although the internal lattice of a crystal – not visible to the naked eye – is fundamental to its energy, its external shape has a bearing too. This outer form does not necessarily reflect the inner structure of a crystal and may subtly effect how energy flows through it.

Shapes may be natural or artificially cut. Their effects are listed below:

- **Ball:** Emits energy equally all round. A window to move through time.

- **Cluster:** Several points on a base create and radiate energy in all directions equally.

- **Double terminated:** Points at both ends emit energy in two directions. Useful for breaking old patterns.

- **Egg:** The gently rounded end focuses and discharges energy and the sharper one pulls it out.

- **Elestial:** Folds, terminations, windows and inner planes radiate flowing energy. This shape absorbs and transmutes negative vibes. Opens insight and change.

- **Generator:** A single six-pointed termination or several points radiating from a fixed base in all directions focuses healing energy or intention, draws people together and attracts abundance.

- **Geode:** Rough outside, beauty and strength within. The 'cave'-like formation amplifies, conserves and slowly releases energy.

- **Phantom:** This enclosed, pointed inner pyramid breaks old patterns and raises vibrations.

- **Point:** Faceted termination. The point out from the body draws off energy. The point in draws in energy. Cleansing and energizing.

- **Sceptre:** A 'head' formed around a central rod is an excellent power and restructuring tool.

✦ **Square:** Consolidates energy, anchors intention and grounds it. Draws off negative energy and transforms it.

✦ **Twin:** Two crystals, usually of equal length, sharing a base draw people together.

✦ **Wand:** A long point, or specially shaped crystal, focuses energy and either draws it off or brings it in. Useful for joining grids.

Exercise: Sensing the effect of shape

✦ Choose a variety of shapes of the same crystal.

✦ Cleanse the crystals (*see page 22*).

✦ Open your palm chakras (*see page 11*).

✦ Place each shape on your palm chakra in turn and allow yourself to feel how the energy radiates from the shape or is drawn in.

✦ Record the results for future reference.

The Mohs scale

The Mohs scale measures the ability of a crystal to withstand surface scratching. Relating to the strength of the chemical bonds that make the structure coherent, it was developed by Friedrich Mohs in 1822, but the ancient geographer Theophrastus referred to scratch resistance in his treatise *On Stones* in 300 BCE.

Small, densely packed atoms create strong bonds and a hard stone. The Mohs scale progresses from 1, the softest crystals, to 10, the hardest. But it isn't a proportional progression, each higher number crystal being exponentially harder than the one before. At 10 on the Mohs scale, Diamond is four times harder than Sapphire, which measures 9, but Sapphire is only twice as hard as Topaz, which is 8.

Each number on the scale scratches itself or anything lower in the table, but won't scratch a higher number. Gemstones need to be at a minimum of 7 to withstand constant wear, but a hard stone isn't necessarily tough or durable.

Number	Test	Example
1	Crumbles easily	Talc
2	Marks with a fingernail	Amber, Selenite
3	Marks with a copper coin	Calcite, Howlite
4	Marks easily with a blade	Fluorite, Rhodochrosite
5	Marks with difficulty	Apatite, Obsidian
6	Marks with a steel file	Rhodonite, Spectrolite
7	Scratches window glass	Agate, Quartz
8	Scratches Quartz	Aquamarine, Topaz
9	Scratches Topaz	Ruby, Sapphire
10	Exceptionally hard	Diamond

SUMMARY

- ✦ Crystals are formed from seven basic geometric shapes plus an anomaly.

- ✦ These shapes have an orderly internal crystal lattice by which a specific crystal is identified.

❖ All crystals generate, store, regulate, transmit and absorb energy, but the fundamental energy-focusing tool is shape.

❖ Crystals may be tumbled, cut or faceted to enhance their appearance.

❖ External shape alters how crystal energy is experienced.

❖ The hardness of crystals is measured by the Mohs scale.

Chapter 6
Nature's paintbox

Some crystals are found in one colour only, others come in several. Colour subtly alters the way they work. Generally, 'hot'-coloured stones – red, orange and yellow ones – stimulate and activate, while 'cool' colours – blue, green and violet – calm, and dark colours ground and transmute.

The colours are created by minerals and trace elements in the mix distorting the crystals' light-refracting properties. Some crystals may also be colour-infused or dyed and heat amended. 'Citrine' produced from heat-treated Amethyst or Smoky Quartz often lacks the dynamic potency of natural Citrine, although it looks brighter. Other crystals, such as Aura Quartzes, are alchemically created.

The magic of light

Colour is a property of light. When light is split by hitting a solid object, it is refracted into the colour spectrum. Colour is produced when a portion of the light is absorbed and the remainder reflected. White results from total reflection, black from total absorption.

Our bodies are extremely sensitive to light. As Sue and Simon Lilly explain in *Healing with Crystals and Chakra Energies*:

> *'What we perceive as colour is simply the brain's way of recognizing the many different energy qualities of light. Every frequency of visible light, each colour, creates changes in us at many different levels, physically, emotionally and mentally. Learning to recognize and use colour with awareness can bring positive and powerful changes into our lives.'*

The light-refracting minerals and trace elements in the chemical mix are what give a crystal its light-reflecting properties, its colour – and its specific properties. Many black crystals, such as Smoky Quartz, have a structure which captures energy as the light is absorbed. This means that the crystal holds onto detrimental energies such as electromagnetic 'smog', or negative thoughts, and transmutes their toxic effect.

In the eye of the beholder

A miniscule amount of an 'alien' substance within the otherwise perfect arrangement of atoms distorts the crystal lattice sufficiently to create colour in the eye of the beholder. When Haematite is present, the crystals may appear red or silvered. Hematite is deep blood-red when raw but magically transforms into silver when polished. Rutile (titanium) turns Quartz pink to create Rose Quartz, but Rutile is also the golden or green threads in Rutilated Quartz and the brilliant blue of Sapphire. Iron also colours Sapphire and stains crystals yellow or pink, Chlorite turns them green and so on.

Colours have general and specific properties, and chakra links and associations through which healing is facilitated (*see Chapter 9*), but colour is not necessarily the only indicator of how a crystal's energy functions. Basic crystals such as Quartz can also be amended by ultraviolet rays from the sun, gamma rays from space or natural Earth radioactivity from uranium, which forms Smoky Quartz. Inclusions and fractures in the crystal lattice also create plays of colour, but these can be replicated artificially.

Artificial colouration

Some crystals are dyed to give an attractive appearance that adds little to the properties of the crystal. Garishly coloured Agate slices have been dyed, as has blue Howlite. Deep black Smoky Quartz has been artificially irradiated, bright yellow Citrine heat-treated. Other crystals are colour-infused, which subtly amps up their properties, and others are alchemicalized to a whole new vibration.

Alchemical crystals

There is a long history of chemical alchemy, rooted in the search to turn base metal into gold. Some of these experiments produced surprising results. Sparkling Goldstone, for instance, is not a natural stone but is created from glass and copper. It is used to attract abundance.

Other alchemical finishes are created by electrostatically adhering gold, indium, titanium and other metals onto the surface of Quartz and similar crystals to create a shimmering effect. Such alchemical crystals, which combine the healing properties of the crystal and the metal, are potent healers.

Crystals that have been dyed or artificially amended to have the same appearance are not.

Case history: The effect of dyeing

When my thyroid ceased working I turned to Tanzine Aura Quartz, alchemicalized from gold and indium, to revive it. Which it did, very successfully. So I recommended it to a friend. After a few days she rang me to say her neck was swollen and lumpy and she felt as though she was being poisoned. Her partner, who owned a crystal shop, enquired of the supplier what could be wrong. 'There must be a problem with the dye' was the answer. Instead of gold and indium being electrostatically bonded, the crystal had been dipped in a vat of purple dye. When my friend obtained a genuine Tanzine Aura, her thyroid too regenerated.

The crystal rainbow

Colour is essentially a vibration of light, and the human body is innately responsive to a whole rainbow of colour and light. The properties of the colours are as follows:

❖ **Silver-grey:** Metallic with alchemical properties of transmutation. Traditionally imparts invisibility, creating excellent journeying crystals.

❖ **Black:** Strongly protective and grounding. Entraps and transmutes negative energies. An excellent detoxifier.

❖ **Brown:** Resonates with the Earth Star chakra. Strongly cleansing and purifying. Grounding and protecting. Absorbs toxic emanations and negative energies and induces stability and centredness.

✤ **Pink:** Exceedingly gentle, carrying the essence of unconditional love. Provides comfort and alleviates anxiety. Excellent 'first aid' emotional healer. Overcomes loss, dispels trauma and promotes forgiveness and attunement to universal love.

✤ **Peach:** Gently energizing. Unites the heart and sacral chakras, combining love with action.

✤ **Red:** Resonates with the base and sacral chakras. Energizes and activates, strengthening the libido and stimulating creativity. Draws off or generates energy as required. Traditionally treats the blood, haemorrhages and inflammation.

✤ **Orange:** Resonates with the sacral chakra. Brings vibrant vitality, stimulates creativity and assertiveness. Grounds projects in the physical world.

✤ **Yellow:** Resonates with the solar plexus and the mind. Instils clarity. Balances emotions and intellect. Golden crystals have long been associated with wealth and abundance.

✤ **Green:** Resonates with the heart chakra. Provides emotional healing and activates compassion. Calming and cleansing, instils tranquillity.

✤ **Green-blue and turquoise:** Activates the third eye, uniting heart and intuition. Induces profound peace and relaxation. Resonates with higher levels of being, stimulates spiritual awareness and metaphysical abilities, drawing higher consciousness down to Earth and anchoring it.

- ❖ **Blue:** Resonates with the throat and third eye chakras. Stimulates self-expression, assists communication, links to the highest states of consciousness. Stimulates intuition and metaphysical abilities, bringing about mystical perception.

- ❖ **Lavender/Lilac/Purple:** Resonates with the higher chakras (*see page 179*) and multi-dimensional realities. Draws spiritual energy into the material plane and opens metaphysical abilities. Encourages service to others.

- ❖ **White:** Resonates with the higher chakras and highest realms of being.

- ❖ **Clear:** A powerful energizer, it purifies and heals the aura and the physical body. Radiates energy out into the environment. Carries the vibration of pure light and higher consciousness.

- ❖ **Combination and bi-coloured crystals:** Create exciting possibilities. Synergizing the qualities of their component colours or crystals and enabling them to work holistically, they are often more effective than the individual parts, with the vibrations being raised to a higher energetic frequency.

Exercise: Sensing colour

You need one crystal of each colour for this exercise.

- ❖ Cleanse your crystals (*see page 22*).

- ❖ Lay the crystals out in a rainbow arc of colour, starting with black and brown at one end and finishing with white and silvery at the other.

❖ Open your palm chakras (*see page 11*).

❖ With your right palm facing down, run it along the arc, starting with the black. Then run your left palm along the arc to ascertain your more sensitive hand. Your palm may tingle or feel hot or cold as it passes through the different energies.

❖ Run your more receptive hand along the arc of colour again. Let yourself feel the energy change as you move from one colour to the next. (Do this with your hand rather than your mind, although you can tell yourself 'This is what black feels like, this is how blue feels,' and so on.)

❖ When you have done this a few times, close your eyes, do it again and let yourself sense which colour you have touched. Open your eyes to check.

❖ Now mix up the colours into a swirl and then run your hand over them with your eyes closed.

❖ Pick up a crystal and sense which colour it is before you open your eyes to check.

❖ Record your results for future reference.

Variations on a Quartz theme

The following crystals are all members of the Quartz family, but their energetic properties are somewhat different due to variations in mineral content and the way in which they were formed. They can be experienced in an exercise that combines shape and colour to develop your sensitivity to crystal energy.

Amethyst

Colour: Lavender to deep purple

Vibration: High to extremely high according to type

Extremely powerful and protective with a high spiritual vibration and strong healing and cleansing powers. Guards against ill-wishing or psychic attack, transmuting the energy. A natural tranquillizer, it blocks geopathic stress and transmutes negative environmental energies. Enhances higher states of consciousness and spiritual awareness.

Anandalite™

Colour: White with rainbow iridescence

Vibration: Exceedingly high

This stone strips you to the bare bones of your soul and rebuilds your energy patterns to accommodate a massive consciousness shift. It deconstructs detrimental energy structures and restructures appropriately. Taking you into the interconnectedness of all life for a quantum uplift, it introduces the limitless possibilities of multi-dimensional being. Generating massive bioscalar waves, it activates the psychic and physical immune systems. Purifying and aligning the whole chakra system to higher frequencies, it prepares the central nervous system for the vibrational shift. (Non-trademarked Anandalite is available as Aurora Quartz.)

Aqua Aura Quartz

Colour: Iridescent dark to light blue (Aura Quartzes are available in other colours)

Vibration: Medium high

Aqua Aura has an intense energy reflecting the alchemical process that bonds gold onto pure Quartz. This Aura Quartz frees you from limitations and creates space for something new. It heals, cleanses and calms the aura, releasing stress and healing 'holes'. It activates the chakras, especially at the throat, where it encourages communication from the heart and strengthens intuitive abilities.

Citrine

Colour: Yellow to greenish yellow (bright yellow is usually heat-treated Amethyst)

Vibration: High

A stone of prosperity. A 'feel-good' abundance crystal. A vibrant energizer, powerful cleanser and regenerator. Warming and highly creative. Absorbs, transmutes and dissipates toxic energy or conflict. Protective for the environment. Raises self-esteem. Natural Citrine has more kick than the heat-amended variety. Kundalini Quartz, natural Citrine from the Congo, activates powerful energies in the body.

Chlorite Quartz

Colour: Green or green pyramids within clear Quartz

Vibration: Earthy

An excellent cleanser and absorber of negative energy. Protects against stress. A useful detoxifier on all levels and extremely beneficial for the environment.

Clear Quartz

Colour: Translucent to water-clear

Vibration: High according to type

An extremely effective energy enhancer and powerful healer. Repairs and replenishes the aura. Radiates energy into the environment or the body. Stimulates the immune system. Regulates physical and mental energy. A deep cleanser on the physical and soul levels. Dissolves karmic seeds. Amplifies intuition. Soothes and protects.

Rose Quartz

Colour: Pale pink

Vibration: High

Gentle and loving, the perfect heart healer and emotional nourisher. Excellent for de-stressing, soothing and stabilizing. Purifies and supports forgiveness. Teaches you how to love and value yourself.

Smoky Quartz

Colour: Brownish grey to blackish (dark black has been artificially irradiated)

Vibration: Earthy to high according to type

An efficient grounding and cleansing crystal. Protective, blocks geopathic stress and electromagnetic smog, assists elimination and detoxification. Teaches how to leave behind anything that no longer serves.

Snow Quartz

Colour: Opaque white

Vibration: Earthy

Gently healing, purifying, revitalizing, calming. Energizes the soul and connects you to your true self. An essential component of ancient stone circles, tombs and megalithic portals that connect to the stars and circulate universal energy. Enhances psychic abilities and calms the mind.

Exercise: Compare and contrast

❖ Choose shaped or raw stones, stones with points and tumbled crystals in different colours from one crystal family such as Quartz (*see above*).

❖ Lay out the cleansed crystals (*see page 22*) in two separate columns on a neutral background, the tumbled on the left and the points, raw or shaped stones on the right, pointing towards you, about two fingers' width apart.

❖ Open the chakras in your palms and your Earth Star chakra (*see page 12*).

❖ With your palm facing down, run each hand in turn down the left-hand column to ascertain your more receptive hand. Your palm may tingle or feel hot or cold.

❖ Now with your eyes closed, run your receptive hand down the column again, letting yourself feel the energy radiating from the crystals. Don't try to *do* anything with your mind, just allow yourself to *feel* the energy through your hands.

❖ Then look at and feel the energy of each crystal in turn, telling yourself, 'This is what Snow Quartz feels like,' and so on. With a little practice you'll soon be able to feel how the basic Quartz energy changes according to the specific type. Snow Quartz has a much slower frequency, for instance, than Clear Quartz or Citrine, which positively fizzes.

❖ Once you've become familiar with the tumbled crystals, turn your attention to the points or other shapes.

❖ A point focuses energy towards you when it is facing you, and channels it away when it is facing outwards. Put each point in turn on your receptive hand first, pointing it up your arm and then down to your fingers. Notice the difference this makes.

- You can move on to putting the point above your head, point down first and then point up.

- And below your feet.

- Record your experience for future reference.

SUMMARY ✍🏻

- Crystals may be formed in one colour or several.

- Colour subtly alters the way crystals work.

- Colour is created by minerals and trace elements within the mix distorting the crystal's light-refracting properties.

- Crystals may be colour-infused or dyed and heat amended.

- Each colour is associated with a chakra in modern crystal healing and has a specific purpose.

Chapter 7
How crystals work

No one can yet say categorically how crystals work, although there have been many suggestions based on vibrational resonance and the water and crystalline content of the human body. Michael Gienger postulates that the power of a crystal to generate light interacts with the cells of the physical body. What is clear is that crystals have an energy field that interacts with any other energy field near it. The interaction of the energy field of a crystal and a human being can, for example, be photographed with a Kirlian camera.

At the simplest level, many crystals contain traces of therapeutic minerals that pass across the skin barrier to bring about physiological changes. Kunzite, as already mentioned, contains lithium, which is used by doctors to medicate depression and bipolar disorders. Crystal users hold Kunzite or place it on their heart and feel uplifted. Similarly the copper content in Malachite alleviates arthritic discomfort – although too much is toxic. It's a matter of maintaining the balance.

However, as Michael Gienger puts it, crystals are actually an information system that radiates energy. Find the right information, and the correct crystal carrier, and the body will be brought back into balance. (*To take this further, see his* Crystal Power, Crystal Healing.)

As we have seen, crystals have an orderliness of structure at the molecular level, with each molecule vibrating at the same rate as all the others. Synchronization takes place so that all the units within the crystal – and every other crystal of the same type – vibrate in unison (a harmonic convergence). Each crystal type has its own fundamental frequency or harmonic note. This creates a coherent, resonant system with a stable frequency template. Coherent systems are difficult to disrupt. Even if there is disharmony or discord nearby, their energy remains stable – and can restore equilibrium to the disrupted energy.

Crystal energy is shaped, amplified and discharged from a crystal's termination and goes out rather like ripples in a pond, creating a rhythmic pattern that pulses in harmony. The basic template can be modified or directed by other energy, such as magnetism, colour waves, intention or the power of thought, passing through it.

Scalar waves may well be the mechanism through which all energetic healing is effected. We'll get to that in a moment.

Everything is energy

At the most basic level, everything is energy. How it manifests is simply a matter of vibrational frequency and the crystalline structure (organic or inorganic) that enfolds it. The human body is no exception. It is a conductive energy system with crystalline structures in and around the blood, lymph and cells and it is repaired and maintained by a complex electrochemical system. In other words, it runs on vibrations. This is not only with regard to physiological processes. Emotions and thoughts also have their own vibration (*see the work of Bruce Lipton and Valerie Hunt*), which go out of kilter during stress and can distort an internal crystal lattice in the body.

Through resonance and entrainment, crystals can restore equilibrium to us. But there is more to it than this. Crystal healing works at a distance. A subtle electromagnetic current passes between a crystal and a person *whether or not they are in physical contact*. What links and activates them is, I believe, consciousness and intention.

Unified field theory

Einstein coined the term 'uniform field theory' when trying to find an overall system that would link all the known forces in the universe with fundamental particle physics. But thousands of years before that the Hindu text the *Mundaka Upanishad* declared:

> *'The sparks, though of one nature with the fire, leap from it, uncounted beings leap from the Everlasting, but these, my son merge into It again. The Everlasting is shapeless, birthless, breathless, mindless, above everything, outside everything, inside everything.'*

This description sounds exactly like the universe from the perspective of a quantum physicist or a modern mystic such as the systems theorist Ervin Laszlo, who says: 'The primary "stuff" of the universe is energy and not matter, and space is neither empty nor passive – it's filled with virtual energies and information.' This also describes crystal energy.

Consciousness: Riding the crest of a wave

Quantum physics suggests energy is not continuous but rather exists as packets of energy – energy that behaves like particles and yet acts like a wave. In discussing consciousness and quantum physics with Jeffrey Mishlove in 1987, theoretical quantum physicist Dr Fred Alan Wolf suggested that consciousness was a huge oceanic wave:

'Consciousness is a huge oceanic wave that washes through everything, and it has ripples and vibrations in it. When there are acts of consciousness, the wave turns into bubbles at that moment, it turns to froth.'

He pointed out that everything, human beings included, was composed of quantum 'froth' and that under an electron microscope we would see:

'A rather bizarre-looking light show, of things popping on and off, vanishing and reappearing, matter created out of nothing and then vanishing. And in that vanishing and creation, an electromagnetic signal is piped from one point to another point.'

This perfectly describes how I perceive crystal energy moving from a crystal to a body, or going out into the future to bring back information (in quantum physics, particles of energy move forwards and backwards, *see below*), or entraining two energy fields.

Entrainment

Entrainment is an energetic interaction. It is defined as 'the synchronization of two or more rhythmic cycles'. In conventional entrainment a smaller energetic field takes on the characteristics of a larger field, but this works both ways, and the larger field can take on the characteristics of the smaller, especially when directed by intention. So, the crystalline structures in the body, especially its flowing tides of blood, lymph, intercellular and synovial fluid, can be entrained into a more perfect energy pattern.

Time and distance have no relevance here. Research has shown that the brainwaves of a healer and the recipient synchronize, or entrain, no matter what the distance. The same may well be true of crystals. A crystal's pulsing energy field has perfect equilibrium and its sympathetic resonance stabilizes a larger field through the energetic synchronization of two crystalline structures.

Quantum crystals

Quantum physics has demonstrated that simultaneous transfer of energy is possible. A particle can be in one place and in another *at the same time* and thought has an instantaneous effect over vast distances. So it seems feasible that crystal energy can travel from a crystal to the recipient.

It is my belief that what unifies and pervades the quantum and the crystal field is consciousness, which is present in and around everything in the universe. Although consciousness studies are increasing, research has not yet turned its attention to crystal consciousness (*but see Mike Eastwood's work with the crystal oversouls*).

Bioscalar waves

Research has, however, been conducted into bioscalar waves. A bioscalar wave is a standing energy field created when two fields interact from different angles and counteract each other so that the field reverts to a 'static state of potentiality'. Research scientist and Professor Emeritus of Physiological Science at UCLA Dr Valerie V. Hunt says that bioscalar waves are 'alive with checked and balanced energies that cancel each other out so that they cannot be measured or evaluated by the instruments in current use'. It is, she says, a 'strong, huge, and yet passive [force]... Only its effects tell us that it exists in space and has power.'

Laser therapy specialist Kalon Prensky describes a scalar wave as 'a non-linear, non-Hertzian, standing wave capable of supporting significant effects including carrying information and inducing higher levels of cellular energy, which greatly enhances the performance and effectiveness of the body and immune system. Additionally it helps to clear cellular memory by shifting polarity, similar to erasing the memory of a cassette tape with a magnet.' He states that 'Scalar Waves travel faster than the speed of light and do not decay over time or distance.' This sounds very much like crystal energy, and depictions of scalar waves look incredibly similar to the crystal energy perceived by a Kirlian camera or the intuitive eye.

Many of the newer crystals such as Anandalite™, Que Sera, Quantum Quattro and Rainbow Mayanite contain concentrated bioscalar energy. All healing crystals probably have this energy within their matrix and generate it through their crystalline structure.

If, as subtle energy researcher Lilli Botchis asserts, 'When the human body enters a scalar wave field, the electromagnetic field of the individual becomes excited [and] this catalyzes the mind/body complex to return to a more optimal state that is representative of its original, natural, electrical matrix form,' we can see how a crystal with its optimal energy pattern might operate on the human – and planetary – energy body.

The effect of bioscalar waves

Research suggests that bioscalar waves assist cell membranes in switching on the most beneficial genetic functions and switching off detrimental patterns encoded within DNA. It has been demonstrated that they directly influence tissue at the microscopic level, bringing about a healing balance. They have been shown to enhance the immune and endocrine systems, stabilize chemical processes, improve the coherence of the biomagnetic field and accelerate healing at all levels. They also release stored emotions and ingrained thoughts from the cellular structures of the body, removing a root cause of psychosomatic dis-ease. Exactly what is claimed for crystal energy and crystal healing.

Integrated holistic healing

Points to consider:

❖ Only one thousand millionth part of our body is matter. The rest is energy.

- ❖ Water is a crystalline structure.

- ❖ The human body is around 57 per cent water, and that water is found in every part of the body, therefore the human body is crystalline.

- ❖ Crystals generate, store and radiate energy.

- ❖ Quantum physics describes energy as controlling matter.

- ❖ Fundamental particles such as electrons influence each other at a considerable distance.

- ❖ Each individual crystal carries the energetic resonance of the crystal type, no matter where in the world it may be.

- ❖ Everything is interconnected in such a way that the smallest piece contains the properties of the whole (the holographic universe).

So it would appear that crystal healing works by bringing back into equilibrium all the separate elements of the body, utilizing universal energetic forces that are encoded into the crystals. The information field of a crystal interacts with that of a human being or a particular environment, with each part influencing the other. This can work at a distance, powered by intention and consciousness. In other words, as Professor John Wheeler puts it, 'In some strange sense the quantum principle tells us that we are dealing with a participatory universe.'

SUMMARY ✍

- At the most basic level, everything is energy.

- How energy manifests is a matter of vibrational frequency.

- The human body is a conductive energy system with crystalline structures.

- Crystals generate minute electrical currents that interact with other currents.

- Crystals contain traces of therapeutic minerals that pass across the skin barrier.

- Our body, our brain and our consciousness are inextricably linked with all other matter in the universe, connected by an invisible network (scalar waves) to each and every thing.

- Through resonance and entrainment, crystals restore equilibrium.

Chapter 8
'A remede against every earthly woe'

Powerful, potent and therapeutic, crystals have many uses. They actively engage with us, adapting themselves and revealing new possibilities. At the most basic level, they interact with our energy field and the environment around us. They help us to manage our wellbeing and protect our space, encourage us to relax and de-stress, cut off energy vampires and block out EMFs that may deplete us. They provide healing for us, our environment and the planet. But they do so much more too – they guide us, expand our awareness and facilitate journeying through other dimensions.

There are many ways of accessing crystal energies and it is vital to find the one that works for you. Once you discover how your own energy functions, you can focus on the ways in which crystals can assist you and the world around you.

Your energy picture

Before we look at how crystals may help you personally, we need to establish a picture of how your energy functions.

Consider the points below to ascertain whether you need assistance with energy management:

❖ On a scale of 1–10, how much energy do I have?

❖ Do I give away too much of my energy?

❖ Do I detach myself after seeing friends, colleagues or clients?

❖ Do I take on negative energy or emotions from people or places?

❖ Am I allowing another person to have undue influence over me?

❖ Do I forget to take enough time for myself?

If you give yourself below a 7 for question 1 and tick two or more other boxes, you need to consider personal energy protection and enhancement. To get a clearer picture, you may also like to ask yourself:

❖ Do particular *places* affect me?

❖ Do I get depleted when I travel on public transport?

❖ Do I always sit or sleep in the same place and feel tired?

If so, you are sensitive to environmental energies and need to protect your space. Chapters 13, 14 and 15 will help you.

What about your boundaries?

Some people have very clear boundaries. They know exactly where they end and someone else begins. They can say 'no'. They have created an interface with which to interact with other people. But there are people who don't really know where they end and someone else begins, which creates problems. If you have loose boundaries and are unable to say 'no' to people or resist their blandishments, you need crystal protection. Ask yourself:

+ Am I able to say 'no'?

+ Do I take on too much for others?

+ Do people dump their troubles on me?

+ Does my aura spread way out from my body? (*See Chapter 9.*)

If so, crystals help you create an interface with which to interact with the outside world. *See Chapter 13.*

De-stressing and disconnection

Other people's demands and expectations can add to your stress levels. De-stressing means finding a calm place inside yourself from which to interact with others. It entails creating clear, appropriate boundaries. Disconnection ensures that your energy is used appropriately and is not squandered by someone other than yourself.

To discover if you need to de-stress and disconnect, consider whether the following statements apply to you:

+ I feel tense and anxious and find it hard to relax.

+ I suffer from disturbed sleep.

+ My everyday life is highly pressured.

+ My working environment is competitive and stressy.

+ A great deal is expected of me.

- I face constant change and uncertainty.

- Other people come to me with their troubles.

- I feel exhausted and worn down in the presence of specific people.

- I feel responsible for others.

- I don't live in the present moment as I worry constantly about the future.

More than three apply to you? Go to chapters 13, 14, 15 and 16 to disconnect and de-stress.

Personal protection

Protection is about keeping your energy high and clear. It creates healthy boundaries and a calm quiet centre. It ensures that other people cannot disturb your equilibrium or draw on your energies. Wearing crystals gives you instant protection, as does placing them in your environment.

Do the following apply to you?

- I easily pick up bad vibes.

- I work or travel in a crowded environment.

- I feel invaded, somehow *not myself*.

- Someone is jealous of me.

- I have upset someone recently.

- I have invisible feelers out, testing the air around me.

- I feel on edge if a friend is angry.

- I work in a highly technological or stressed environment.

✦ People gravitate to me with their troubles.

✦ I was born under the zodiac sign of Cancer, Scorpio or Pisces.

If more than half do, personal protection will help. Go to Chapter 13.

Healing – Body

Again, think about whether the following statements are true for you:

✦ I am perpetually tired, listless, drained.

✦ I have a chronic illness.

✦ I get unexplained aches and pains.

✦ I react physically to outside stimuli or pollutants.

You'll find assistance with all of these in chapters 10 and 13.

Healing – Mind

Think about whether the following statements are true for you:

✦ I'm afraid to relax.

✦ I worry excessively about what is going on in the world.

✦ I am obsessed with thoughts of failure or loss.

✦ Things churn round and round in my mind.

✦ I've got my head in the clouds.

✦ I have nightmares and insomnia.

- ❖   I am anxious, nervy, on edge.

You'll find assistance in chapters 12 and 13.

Healing – Psyche

Think about whether the following statements are true for you:

- ❖   I cry easily.
- ❖   I feel overwhelmed by old emotions or thoughts.
- ❖   I feel depressed and hopeless.
- ❖   I can't take 'me time' without feeling guilty.
- ❖   I get other people's baggage dumped on me.
- ❖   Feeling upset results in physical illness.

You'll find chapters 11, 12 and 13 of assistance.

Space clearing and environmental healing

Think about whether the following statements are true for you:

- ❖   Particular places affect me.
- ❖   I get tired in certain areas.
- ❖   I am surrounded by technology.
- ❖   I live in an area of trauma or threat.
- ❖   There is a history of conflict in my land.
- ❖   I want to assist the Earth.

If so, space and environmental healing will help you. Go to chapters 14 and 15.

Metaphysical applications

Think about whether the following statements are true for you:

❖ I want to take my crystal experience to a new level.

❖ I'd like to meditate with my crystals.

❖ I'd like to journey with my crystals.

❖ I need guidance on my future.

❖ I want to know about my birthstone.

❖ I want to meet my guardian angel.

You can explore all these in chapters 16, 17, 18, 19 and 20.

Do crystals work for everyone?

Now you have an idea of how crystals can help you, let's look at how you can interact with them.

Some people are naturally sensitive to crystal energy and feel it the instant they come into contact with their first crystal. For others it takes time and effort to make the connection. Crystal energy, as with all information received intuitively, isn't always 100 per cent effective. The energy interacts with your own energy field (your aura) and this may sometimes be too closed for the energy to make an impression. It also bumps up against ingrained beliefs or hopes that distort it. Other factors may operate too. Chakras may be blocked, for instance (*see Chapter 9*).

There may also be reasons why healing or divination is not appropriate at a particular time; see my *The Book of Why* to discover more about this. You also need to experiment to find exactly the right crystals for you. You can improve your hit rate, however, by:

✤ listening to your body and inner knowing

✤ avoiding scepticism and self-doubt

✤ letting go of wishful thinking and staying with what is

✤ clarifying signs and images before jumping to conclusions

✤ honing your abilities

Different ways of sensing

People attune to crystal energy in different ways. Information can be received through the physical body or the intuitive senses.

Modes of sensing

✤ hearing (aural)

✤ seeing (visual)

✤ sensing (kinaesthetic)

✤ feeling (kinaesthetic)

✤ knowing (kinaesthetic)

✤ smelling (kinaesthetic-sensate)

✤ through the muscles or skin (kinaesthetic-sensate)

These modes govern the way in which your sensitivity to crystal energy functions. Most people use a combination of two or more. Paying too much attention to one mode of sensing may overwhelm the subtle signals you would otherwise receive via a different mode. When you are working through the activities in this book, try deliberately switching modes by focusing your attention on the inner eye or ear, your senses or your body. The more modes that are available to you, the more acute your sensitivity becomes.

But first, how does your awareness naturally function?

Which sensing mode do you use?

✦ I'm stimulated by patterns, colour, images, gestures and body language.

✦ I find it easy to visualize.

✦ I think in pictures.

✦ I have vivid Technicolor dreams.

✦ My eyes to go slightly out of focus and I 'see' energy from the corner of my eye.

✦ I use phrases like 'I don't quite see what you mean.'

If more than half of these apply to you, you routinely use the visual mode to process information. You *see*, rather than *sense*, the energy of your crystals and the effect they have. Your crystal experience is enhanced through the use of softly focused eyes, vivid imagery, mandalas or grids and quiet observation.

Seeing is facilitated by drawing crystal energy or feeling a crystal in your palm. Try focusing on a crystal ball or scrying mirror. Use crystal cards or cast the stones.

What about the following statements?

- ✦ I am powerfully affected by words, sounds and music.
- ✦ I find myself asking, 'Could you repeat that?'
- ✦ I say, 'I didn't quite catch that.'
- ✦ I close my eyes and listen when I want to concentrate.
- ✦ I tilt my head to one side with a particular ear forward.

If you agree with them, your mode of sensing is auditory. You *hear* crystal energy, maybe as a rushing or bubbling sound, or experience a voice in your inner ear guiding you. The ear you point forward is your intuitive ear.

Your crystal experience is enhanced by chanting, mantras, background music, and focused sounds such as a Tibetan bowl or cymbals. Try holding a crystal to your ear.

How about the following?

- ✦ I am strongly affected by smell, touch, gesture and sensation.
- ✦ My body feels like a receiver that shivers or quivers.
- ✦ I get nausea or excitement in my gut in response to places or people.
- ✦ I make statements like 'I can't quite get a grip on that.'
- ✦ I say, 'My gut tells me.'

✦ I say, 'I'm feeling a little blue today.'

If these are you, you use the kinaesthetic/sensate mode to process crystal information.

Your crystal experience is enhanced – or smothered – by incense or strong perfumes. Try tracing symbols and grids, making ritual gestures and body movements. Massage scented oils gently over your third eye. Sandalwood and frankincense have been prized over millennia for their consciousness-enhancing effects.

Smell and crystal awareness

The olfactory sense is often overlooked in crystal work and yet it is a powerful and evocative form of communication. Some crystals have a distinctive smell of their own. As might be expected, Rain Forest Jasper smells of the forest and Ocean Jasper of the sea, but iron-rich stones also have a distinctive aroma. In crystal divination, smells that belong to a certain location alert you to events occurring there, even if you are many miles away. In healing, sour odours point to blockages and dis-ease.

Facilitating crystal sensitivity

Scientific research has shown that altered states of consciousness and deep relaxation help intuitive awareness to function efficiently. The mind needs to be slightly displaced, disengaged from the everyday, to have moved from functional perception to intuitive perception – an older and more natural way of perceiving the world.

Your body might be talking to you right now, but are you listening? Are you trying to figure things out? If so, stop the mind chatter and listen to the still voice from within yourself. Take the time to sit down quietly, contemplate your crystal and ask for guidance (*see chapters 2 and 16*). Then it's a case of asking the right kind of questions instead of constantly questioning. After that, trust is the quickest way to get your crystal sensitivity moving.

Getting out of your own way assists awareness. Stand aside placidly, put aside wishful thinking, prejudices, hopes and expectations, and allow your sensitivity to make itself felt in its unique way.

Research has shown that you can improve your metaphysical sensitivity by:

◆ muscle relaxation

◆ reduced sensory input

◆ cortical arousal – that is, remaining attentive

◆ spontaneous mental processes, especially imagery

◆ a goal or a need to communicate

◆ staying present in the moment

◆ sustained emotional wellbeing

◆ a calm, clear-headed and focused approach

It has also been demonstrated that ten crucial factors affect the operation of intuition:

✦ **An open mind:** An open mind looks at the evidence, assesses it dispassionately and accepts or rejects it on the basis of what is. But if you remain too detached, you won't access the subliminal perceptions on which crystal sensitivity is based.

✦ **Belief:** If you believe you sense crystal energy, something magical happens: your inner knowing works on your behalf.

✦ **Desire:** You must want an outcome, but beware of trying too hard. Emotional investment in the outcome actually inhibits awareness.

✦ **Focused intention:** Intention focuses the will and sets things in motion.

✦ **Expectation:** The expectation that you will quickly master an activity or receive an answer allows your inner knowing to flourish.

✦ **A positive attitude:** Maintaining a positive attitude enhances your awareness.

✦ **The ability to move out of everyday awareness:** Sensitivity functions best in a state of heightened awareness and low sensory input. This is achieved by withdrawing your awareness from the outside world and focusing your attention on yourself or your crystal.

✦ **Trust:** You need to trust yourself, the guidance you receive and the process. However, this trust is not a naïve, gullible state. You also need to be able to discriminate.

❖ **Common sense:** Your common sense helps you to keep your feet on the ground.

❖ **Willingness to take risks:** Using your crystal sensitivity, certainly in the initial stages, may feel unsettling. The willingness to take a risk is vital if you are to expand your awareness.

Exercise: Exercising your sensory mode

❖ Pick up a cleansed crystal (*see page 22*) and hold it in your hands. Examine it carefully, letting your eye follow its planes and flaws and going deep within if it is translucent. Does it stimulate pictures in your mind?

❖ Now pick up a cleansed crystal and put it to your ear. Do you hear the energy moving?

❖ Pick up a cleansed crystal and sniff it. Does it remind you of anything?

❖ Pick up a cleansed crystal and trace a triangle in the air with it. Sense the energetic shape it leaves behind.

❖ Ask yourself which was easiest for you. Did this accord with the sensing mode you had identified above?

Heal yourself, heal your world

Once you have experienced crystal energy for yourself, you will find that as you heal, the environment around you benefits too. That includes other people. When one person makes an energetic shift, everyone can. However, crystals can be directly applied to the external world to bring healing and balance (*see Chapter 15*). Programming a Rose Quartz or Eye of the Storm (Judy's Jasper) sends peace to an area, for instance. We will look at applications of crystals in the next part of this book.

SUMMARY ✍

- ❖ At the most basic level, crystals interact with your energy field and the environment around you.

- ❖ Once you discover how your own energy functions, you can focus on the ways in which crystals can assist.

- ❖ Crystals help you to manage your wellbeing, protect your space, de-stress, cut off energy vampires and block out EMFs.

- ❖ The best-known crystal application is holistic healing, which balances mind, body and spirit.

Part II
CRYSTAL APPLICATIONS

Now that you've learned how crystals work and what they can do, it's time to learn how to use them to enhance your life.

Chapter 9

Crystals, the aura and the chakras

Vortices for the reception or transmission of subtle energy, chakras link the subtle energy bodies (the aura) that surround and interpenetrate the physical body and mediate energy flow. They help the body assimilate *Qi*, the life force, and assist communication between the different dimensions of being: physical, emotional, mental, karmic, metaphysical, cosmic and spiritual. Healthy chakras create a healthy body and blockages can be dissolved with crystals.

The aura: The biomagnetic sheath

A measurable biomagnetic energetic sheath that surrounds the physical body, the aura has many layers. These interpenetrate and, to the psychic eye, look like misty colours weaving in and out. Any physical, emotional, mental or spiritual dis-ease shows up as a dark patch or broken energy lines in the aura.

If your aura extends too far out, people interpenetrate it and pull on your energy or infuse you with negativity. If it's too close, it doesn't have room to filter energies before they reach you. A comfortable distance is about arm's length all around your body, but if you feel 'invaded', pull your aura in closer and protect it with a crystal (*see below*). Blockages, holes or 'tears' in your auric field leave you open to subtle energetic invasion, but a crystal quickly cleanses and repairs the field or the chakra linkage point.

Exercise: Repairing your aura

❖ Stand comfortably so you can reach all around yourself (sit if you find this easier).

❖ Take a cleansed Clear Quartz, Flint or Selenite crystal and, starting at arm's length above your head, gently brush all over your aura with it.

❖ If the crystal hesitates or drops inwards, or you feel a cold patch or sense a hook or a cord-like obstruction anywhere, hold the crystal in that place and ask it to dissolve the hook and repair the hole with light. Spiralling the crystal out, flicking it and spiralling it back in helps this process.

❖ When you've checked out the outer levels of your aura, work a little more closely in towards your body, and then move closer still until you're sure your aura is healthy and whole.

Crystals for the aura

Flint

Vibration: Earthy

A basic, earthy stone, Flint is made from the decomposed and cemented bodies of marine creatures. It cleanses and filters energy and opens a portal to other worlds.

Selenite

Vibration: Extremely high

Physiological correspondences: The biochemical, chemical and electrical processes within the cells and the organs that make up the physical body

Crystallized divine light, ethereal white Selenite occupies the space between light and matter. It's excellent for repairing and re-energizing the aura. This stone holds a deep inner peace and meditating with it takes you into pure light and also creates a protective grid around your home, as it does not allow outside influences to penetrate. A large piece within the house ensures a peaceful atmosphere.

Other auric crystals include:

* **For cleansing:** Amber, Anandalite™, Bloodstone, Green Jasper, Herkimer Diamond, Quartz or Smoky Quartz.

* **For protection:** Amber, Amethyst, Apache Tear, Black Tourmaline, Diamond, Labradorite, Quartz or Shattuckite with Ajoite (wear continuously).

* **For alignment:** To align your aura with your physical body, place Amber over your head or solar plexus. To align your aura spiritually, place Labradorite over your head.

* **For repair:** To repair holes, use Amethyst, Anandalite™, Aqua Aura, Green Tourmaline, Quartz or Selenite.

The chakras: Vital energy links

In recent times, the chakras have been simplified to seven main energy points, but, as ancient diagrams show, there are many more, and additional chakras are now coming online as our consciousness expands.

Each chakra is assigned a colour, but the colours used today are a modern attribution. Crystals with older chakra designations may not conform to this system and other colours of crystals can be equally effective. Follow the crystal–chakra attribution rather than sticking with a colour when exploring what works for you.

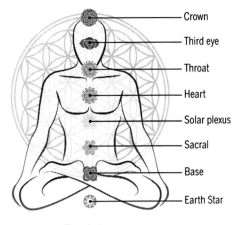

Crown
Third eye
Throat
Heart
Solar plexus
Sacral
Base
Earth Star

The chakras

Everyday connections

Each chakra links to a specific area of life and to various organs and conditions. Chakras below the waist are primarily physical, although blockages affect endocrine gland functioning, with resultant personality traits. Those in the upper torso are for the most part aligned to emotional functioning and the psyche. Blockages here create psychosomatic conditions. Those in the head function on a mental and metaphysical intuitive/spiritual basis, but blockages here also have physical repercussions.

Blown chakras

If a chakra is too open, it is known as a 'blown' chakra. This leads to negative conditions forming. A blown chakra is particularly vulnerable to outside influences, as there is no protection or filtering. Similarly, a chakra can be stuck in the closed position, which also leads to negative qualities manifesting. A chakra may be blocked because of our own past experiences or because other people 'put a block' on it – that is, they control us, don't want us to sense what is really going on, and so on.

Chakra imbalances can be rectified and chakras harmonized by placing crystals of the appropriate vibration over the chakras for 10 to 15 minutes (*see pages 93, 98 and 182*).

Chakra spin

To a psychic eye, chakras look like whirling pools of light. Despite what you may read in books, individual chakras have their own direction of spin, and reversing yours may not be appropriate, so allow your intuition – or a crystal – to know what is appropriate. Spiralling a crystal out from a chakra opens and cleanses it. Spiralling back in re-energizes and seals it. Let your intuition tell you the direction in which to move the crystal. You may need to cleanse it in between.

Chakra	Colour	Function
Earth Star	brown	grounding and protection
Base	red	energizing and survival
Sacral	orange	creation and activation
Solar plexus	yellow	nurturing and feeling
Heart	green	healing emotional distress, radiating love
Throat	blue	communication, self-expression
Third eye	indigo	metaphysical attunement
Crown	white/purple	intuition and higher awareness

Closing chakras

Chakras such as the third eye need to be closed down at times if you are not to be overwhelmed by psychic impressions. Similarly, you need to protect your solar plexus at times of strong emotion.

Placing your hand over the site closes a chakra, as does placing a piece of Flint over it.

Keeping your Earth Star chakra open helps to ground your energies unless you are in an area with disturbed or toxic Earth energies.

High-vibration chakras

High-vibration chakras are coming online now as energy shifts occur. These chakras assist in assimilating changing frequencies and exploring other dimensions (*see Chapter 16*).

Healing through the chakras

Chakric pathways to health

Traditionally physical illness starts in one of four ways (*see Chapter 10*), but we can add a fifth: chakra blockages. When the chakras are invaded or disturbed, or weak or damaged, they cannot mediate the flow of life force around the body, leaving the physical immune system depleted and the endocrine system affected.

To crystal healers, dis-ease (as opposed to injury) starts in the aura and chakras. It is the state that results from physical imbalances, blocked feelings, suppressed emotions and toxic thinking. If not reversed, it moves from the subtle to the physical; see my *The Book of Why* for further details. In addition, the aura and the chakras carry not only present life dis-ease and emotional imprints but also past-life attitudes and wounds that affect how the present-life physical body functions.

Dis-ease can be addressed by bringing the chakras and the subtle bodies into an equilibrium that passes into the physical body. However, crystal energies also work directly on the site of the pain, disturbance or dis-ease (*see chapters 10, 11 and 12*).

The chakras and physiology

These are the correspondences between the chakras and the areas of the body (there are some crossovers in certain areas):

❖ **Base chakra:** Adrenals, bladder and elimination system, gonads, immune system, kidneys, lower back, lower extremities, lymph system, prostate gland, rectum, skeletal system (teeth and bones), veins, sense of smell

✦ **Sacral chakra:** Bladder and elimination system, gallbladder, immune system, kidneys, lumbar and pelvic region, ovaries, spleen, testes, uterus, sense of taste

✦ **Solar plexus chakra:** Adrenals, digestion, liver, lymphatic system, metabolism, pancreas, skin, small intestine, stomach, eyesight

✦ **Heart chakra:** Chest, circulation, heart, lungs, shoulders, thymus, sense of touch

✦ **Throat chakra:** Ears, nervous system, nose, respiratory system, sinuses, skin, throat, thyroid, tongue, tonsils, speech and body language

✦ **Third eye chakra:** Brain, ears, eyes, neurological system, pineal gland, scalp, sinuses, hearing

✦ **Crown chakra:** Brain, central nervous system, hair, hypothalamus, pituitary gland, spine

Chakra crystals

✦ **Earth Star chakra:** Boji Stone, Brown Jasper, Cuprite, Fire Agate, Flint, Graphic Smoky Quartz in Feldspar, Haematite, Mahogany Obsidian, Rhodonite, Smoky Quartz, Smoky Elestial Quartz, Tourmaline

✦ **Base chakra:** Bloodstone, Carnelian, Cuprite, Fire Agate, Garnet, Graphic Smoky Quartz, Menalite, Pink Tourmaline, Red Calcite, Red Jasper, Smoky Quartz

✦ **Sacral chakra:** Blue Jasper, Citrine, Menalite, Orange Calcite, Orange Carnelian, Que Sera, Topaz

- **Solar plexus chakra:** Citrine, Golden Beryl, Jasper, Malachite, Rhodochrosite, Tiger's Eye, Yellow Tourmaline

- **Heart chakra:** Aventurine, Chrysocolla, Danburite, Green Jasper, Green Quartz, Green Tourmaline, Jade, Jadeite, Kunzite, Morganite, Muscovite, Pink Tourmaline, Rhodochrosite, Rhodonite, Rose Quartz, Ruby, Tugtupite, Variscite, Watermelon Tourmaline

- **Throat chakra:** Amber, Amethyst, Aquamarine, Blue Lace Agate, Kunzite, Lepidolite, Topaz, Tourmaline, Turquoise

- **Third eye chakra:** Apophyllite, Aquamarine, Azurite, Herkimer Diamond, Iolite, Kunzite, Lapis Lazuli, Lepidolite, Malachite with Azurite, Moldavite, Preseli Bluestone, Purple Fluorite, Royal Sapphire, Sodalite, Yellow Labradorite

- **Crown chakra:** Angelite, Clear Tourmaline, Golden Beryl, Larimar, Lepidolite, Moldavite, Quartz, Petalite, Phenacite, Purple Jasper, Purple Sapphire, Selenite

- **To cleanse and align all the chakras:** Anandalite™, Citrine, Graphic Smoky Quartz, Kyanite, Quantum Quattro, Quartz, Sunstone

- **To align chakras with the physical body:** Amber, Graphic Smoky Quartz, Que Sera

- **To dissolve blockages:** Bloodstone, Clear Quartz, Graphic Smoky Quartz, Lapis Lazuli, Rainbow Mayanite

- **For blown chakras and chakra repair:** Fire Agate, Graphic Smoky Quartz, Que Sera, Rainbow Mayanite

- **For cleansing:** Amethyst, Anandalite™, Bloodstone,

Calcite, Citrine, Gold and Silver Healer, Graphic Smoky Quartz, Quartz, Que Sera, Rainbow Mayanite, Tourmaline wand

✦ **To prevent energy leakage:** Ajoite with Shattuckite, Graphic Smoky Quartz, Green Aventurine, Labradorite, Quartz, Que Sera

✦ **For protection:** Apache Tear, Graphic Smoky Quartz, Jet, Labradorite, Quartz

✦ **For strengthening:** Graphic Smoky Quartz, Magnetite (Lodestone), Quartz, Que Sera

Crystal chakra healing

Blockages or imbalances in the chakras are treated by placing crystals on the chakra in question. An appropriate crystal redresses any imbalance and brings the chakra back into equilibrium.

Colour is not the only indicator of how a crystal's energy functions, or what a chakra requires. Placing a crystal on a chakra according to whether it needs stimulating or sedating can be more beneficial than using the traditional chakra colours, as if a chakra is overactive it may need calming *or* stimulating to work appropriately, or, if blocked, it will need activating. A stimulating and a sedating crystal placed together on the same chakra will neutralize the effect of each, but placed one after the other as appropriate will restore balance.

Dowsing (*see page 17*) or sensing with your palm chakras pinpoints which chakras need balancing and which need stimulating or sedating, but you can also use a crystal, such as a Lemurian Seed or Indicolite (Blue) Tourmaline, which 'jumps', twitches or tingles at a site of imbalance.

If you are using a crystal with a point, placing it with the point facing outwards will draw negative energy away from the body, and with the point facing in will draw energy into the body.

You can do a complete chakra cleanse and recharge (*see page 103*) or cleanse a specific chakra if you identify an issue associated with that chakra. Throat or lung conditions, for instance, respond to treating the throat chakra and abdominal distress to treating the base or sacral chakras. We look further at this in Chapter 10.

A chakra that is closed or blocked feels energy-less, lifeless. One that is too open or blown feels buzzy and whizzy, with energy flying off in all directions. A balanced chakra has a calm, centred energy with a measured spin. Each chakra functions holistically and we'll be looking at some of them in the following chapters, but first we'll reconnect to an essential grounding chakra and explore two of the more physically linked chakras.

The Earth Star chakra

Location: Beneath your feet

The sphere of everyday reality and groundedness. Imbalances or blockages lead to discomfort in the physical body, feelings of helplessness and the inability to function practically in the world, also to picking up adverse environmental factors such as geopathic stress and toxic pollutants. When properly functioning, the chakra filters these out.

Typical dis-eases are lethargic: Arthritis, autoimmune diseases, cancer, depression, ME, muscular disorders, psychiatric disturbances

The base chakra

Location: The base of the spine/perineum

The sphere of basic survival instincts and security issues, the 'fight or flight' response. Imbalances lead to sexual disturbances and feelings of stuckness, anger, impotence and frustration and the inability to let go.

Typical dis-eases can be constant low-level ones or flare up suddenly: Autoimmune diseases, bipolar disorder, chronic lower back pain, glandular disturbances, personality and anxiety disorders, renal, reproductive or rectal disorders such as fluid retention/constipation (diarrhoea if the chakra is blown), stiffness in the joints, varicose veins or hernias

The sacral chakra

Location: Halfway between the belly button and the base of the pubic bone

The sphere of creativity, fertility and acceptance of yourself as a powerful and sexual being. Imbalances lead to infertility and blocked creativity. The sacral chakra is where 'hooks' from other people may make themselves felt, particularly from sexual encounters.

Typical dis-eases are toxic and psychosomatic: Addictions, allergies, chronic back pain, diabetes, eating disorders, impotence, infertility, liver or intestinal dysfunction including irritable bowel syndrome, PMT and muscle cramps, reproductive blockages or diseases, urinary infections

Exercise: Sensing blockages and balancing the chakras

Select a variety of crystals (*see page 98*). You could work with a friend on this activity, checking out each other's chakras.

✦ Open your palm chakras (*see page 11*). Sit in an upright chair to begin with (or lie down if working with a friend). If you are using your palm to check out the chakras, hold it towards a chakra about a hand's breadth out from your body. If you are dowsing to check the chakras, hold the pendulum level with the chakra, but use your palm to sense the energy first.

✦ Begin with the Earth Star chakra beneath your feet. Hold the pendulum or your palm just above your feet.

✦ Sense the energy. Is it lifeless, or buzzy, spinning, whirling off? Does it need stimulating or sedating? (Let your intuition help you to know the answer to this.) If the chakra feels particularly 'sticky', spiral the crystal out, cleanse it and then spiral it in again.

✦ Place different crystals between your feet in turn and note the change in energy. When you find the right crystal to balance the chakra (you will sense this), leave it in place. Picture light and energy radiating out from the crystal into the Earth Star chakra for two or three minutes. Be aware that the chakra is being cleansed and its spin regulated. It will then anchor you into incarnation and mediate the vibration of Earth.

✦ Check out the base chakra and place or tape a red or other appropriate crystal on it. Picture light and energy radiating out from the crystal into the chakra for a few moments.

✦ Place or tape an orange or other appropriate crystal on your sacral chakra, just below the navel. Feel the cleansing process.

✦ Place a yellow or other appropriate crystal on your solar plexus.

✦ Place a green or other appropriate crystal on your heart.

✦ Place a blue or other appropriate crystal on your throat.

✦ Place an indigo or other appropriate crystal on your brow.

✦ Place a lilac-purple crystal on your crown.

✦ Place a white or other appropriate crystal (point facing down if it has one) above your head.

✦ Now take your attention slowly from the soles of your feet up the midline of your body, feeling how each chakra has become balanced and harmonized.

✦ Remain still and relaxed, breathing deep down into your belly and counting to seven before you exhale. As you breathe in and hold, feel the energy of the crystals re-energizing the chakras and radiating out through your whole being.

✦ When you feel ready, gather your crystals up, starting from above the crown. As you reach the Earth Star, be aware of a grounding cord anchoring you to the Earth and to your physical body.

✦ Cleanse the crystals thoroughly (*see page 22*).

Case history: Menalite for conception

Anna was a young woman who longed to have a baby but had failed to conceive for over three years. She was depressed and anxious and she and her husband were about to undergo tests. Sensing lower chakra blockages, I gave her a Menalite and suggested she kept it in her pocket during the day (where it would radiate into the belly chakras) and put it under her pillow at night. I had used this stone, which is traditionally associated with conception and birth, successfully with several other women.

When next I saw Anna, she was pregnant. She had conceived that very night. She was still using the Menalite to help her through the pregnancy and would do so with the birth.

Menalite

Vibration: Earthy

Chakras: Base and sacral

Physiological correspondences: Breasts, hormonal-endocrine systems and the female reproductive system

Menalite guides a soul as it incarnates. It energetically guards both mother and unborn child, bringing them safely through pregnancy to birth, then encourages lactation and mother–child bonding. Solidifying the core energy field, it is also a powerful healer during female transitions such as puberty and menopause. It adjusts and rebalances the subtle hormonal system and provides psychological support, and during night sweats or hot flushes it draws out the heat and moisture, promoting restful sleep.

SUMMARY ✍

- The aura is a measurable biomagnetic energetic sheath that surrounds the physical body.

- Crystals can be used to repair the aura.

- Chakras are vortices for the reception or transmission of subtle energy.

- Chakras help the body assimilate *Qi*, the life force, and assist communication between different dimensions of being.

- Healthy chakras create a healthy body. Crystals can assist.

- Chakras are traditionally linked to certain colours, although different coloured crystals may well be beneficial for chakras.

Chapter 10
Holistic healing: Body

We have already explored the effect of chakra blockages on wellbeing and in the next chapter we'll look at psychosomatic dis-ease. Now it is time to turn our attention to the body itself. In the medical model, illnesses are caused by:

❖ the invasion of pathogens such as bacteria or viruses

❖ direct insult or injury to the body

❖ a disturbance in the organs, cells or DNA

❖ the psychosomatic effect of the mind and the emotions

In the context of crystal healing, illness is a dis-ease, the final manifestation of spiritual, environmental, psychological, karmic, emotional or mental imbalance, distress or blockage. In holistic healing, deeper causes are considered along with the presenting symptom.

Holistic healing

Holistic healing means bringing mind, body and spirit back into balance for maximum wellbeing. It does not imply a cure.

Crystals act holistically to balance mind, body and spirit. They focus and direct energy to a specific point on the body or to an emotional or mental blockage. Dis-ease is gently dissolved, imbalance corrected, equilibrium restored.

Crystals can be used to alleviate symptoms, but it is preferable to work with the underlying cause. So, if your symptom is a digestive problem, for example, you could choose a Citrine point to assist. Laying it on your abdomen or wearing it on your little finger (which connects to the small intestine energetic meridian) could calm your digestion. The crystal would work directly on the physical body or on the solar plexus chakra (blockages here can cause digestive problems), but on an emotional and mental level, digestive problems often relate to a lack of abundance, and that also needs to be addressed. Wearing a Citrine re-energizes you, however. It stimulates your motivation and creativity and opens the way for abundance. Going deeper, to a spiritual level, fears around money often stem from a feeling of being unsupported by the universe. This fear is not merely psychosomatic dis-ease, it is spiritual disconnection. This could also be healed through the use of the Citrine, as its ability to activate the crown chakra, from which spiritual connection is made, could strengthen your trust in the universe.

Illness or disability as a means of soul growth

Some dis-eases, both physical and psychological, have been deliberately taken on at a soul level and are actually vehicles for soul growth, either for ourselves or someone else. 'Healing' these dis-eases requires an understanding of the dynamics and the soul gifts that are offered by the experience. This is outside the sphere of this book, but it is worth bearing in mind if you are dealing with any chronic dis-ease or disability; see my *The Book of Why* for more information. An intuitive crystal healer can assist.

Crystal healing applications

Subtle meridians and energetic pathways run through the body, carrying *Qi*, life force energy. This flow can be heightened or sedated with crystals for maximum wellbeing. Crystals also have useful pain-relieving properties and some, such as Shungite, have been shown to be antibacterial and antiviral and can be utilized as a crystal essence or crystal water (*see page 119*).

In the simplest application of crystal healing, the body can be brought back into balance by placing an appropriate crystal over the site of pain or discomfort, or over an organ. Or, if you are already familiar with the body's meridian system, utilize this. Brief crystal and organ connections are given below, but for further assistance, see my *Crystal Prescriptions* or the *Crystal Bibles*, and if in doubt at any time, consult a qualified crystal healer.

As an example of what crystals can do for the physical body, try this instant energy boost:

Exercise: Getting an instant energy boost

Place a Carnelian over your sacral chakra for a few minutes or Red Jasper over your base and it will power up your whole system, giving you an instant energy boost.

Crystal first aid

Shamans and crystal therapists are familiar with the ability of crystals to focus sound and light vibrations into a concentrated ray, which is then applied for healing. Rotating a crystal wand on the skin causes compression, which releases a focused beam to the organ beneath. However, ancient healers knew that there were crystals that sedated an overactive organ or stimulated a sluggish one. Red Jasper, for instance, stimulates, while cool green Eye of the Storm sedates and detoxes before stimulating the flow of *Qi*. Magnetite, with its positive and negative charge, sedates or stimulates as required.

Some crystals heal quickly, but may provoke a healing challenge, whilst others work more slowly. For this reason it is sensible to consult a crystal healer. However, crystals are useful as a 'first aid' measure. Simply place an appropriate one (dowse for this or check in *Crystal Prescriptions*) over the site.

Crystal first aid kit

Amethyst
Qualities: Cleansing, opening, protecting, stabilizing, tranquillizing, transmuting
Organs: Brain, intestines, lungs
Gland: Pineal
Systems: Digestive, endocrine, immune, metabolic, nervous, skeletal, subtle bodies
Chakras: Brow, crown, throat

Bloodstone
Qualities: Cleansing, protecting, revitalizing
Organs: Bladder, intestines, kidneys, liver, spleen
Gland: Thymus
Systems: Circulatory, immune, lymphatic, metabolic
Chakras: Base and heart

Blue Lace Agate
Qualities: Activating, calming, cooling, opening
Organs: Brain, pancreas, throat
Glands: Parathyroid, thyroid
Systems: Lymphatic, nervous, skeletal
Chakra: Throat

Carnelian
Qualities: Cleansing, energizing, grounding, stabilizing, stimulating
Organs: Intestines, kidneys, reproductive organs
Glands: Adrenals
Systems: Metabolic, reproductive
Chakras: Base, sacral and spleen

Clear Quartz
Qualities: Absorbing, balancing, energizing, purifying, regulating; releases and stores energy
Organs: All
Glands: Pineal and pituitary
Systems: Auric, immune
Chakras: All

Golden Healer

Qualities: Master healer, powerful regeneration for all the body and the spirit

Organs: All

Glands: All

Systems: All

Chakras: All, especially those from the solar plexus upwards

Green Aventurine

Qualities: Activating, cleansing, regulating, stabilizing

Organs: Adrenals, eyes, heart, lungs, sinuses

Gland: Thymus

Systems: Connective tissue, mental, muscular, nervous, urogenital

Chakras: Heart, spleen

Quantum Quattro

Qualities: Detoxifies, heals psychosomatic causes of dis-ease, protects, restores equilibrium, strengthens the immune system and DNA, tones and brings the body back into balance

Organs: All

Glands: All, especially the thymus

Systems: All

Chakras: All

Que Sera

Qualities: Powerful synergistic healing for all the body, especially the immune system

Organs: All

Glands: All, especially the thymus

Systems: All
Chakras: All

Rose Quartz

Qualities: Assimilating, forgiving, releasing, restoring, sedating
Organs: Genitals, heart, kidneys, liver, lungs
Glands: Adrenals, thymus
Systems: Circulatory, lymphatic
Chakra: Heart

Shungite

Qualities: Research suggests that Shungite assists cellular metabolism, neurotransmitters, digestive, filtration and immune systems, enhances enzyme production and provides pain relief. It is an antibacterial, antihistamine, anti-inflammatory, antioxidant and detoxifier.
Organs: All
Glands: All
Systems: All
Chakra: Base, Earth Star and heart

Shungite water

Qualities: Used for allergies, arthritis and osteoarthritis, asthma, autoimmune diseases, blood disorders, burns, cardiovascular diseases, chronic fatigue syndrome, diabetes, gallbladder dysfunction, gastric disturbances, kidney and liver disorders, pancreatic disorders and sore throats. (*To make Shungite water, see page 120.*)

Smoky Quartz
Qualities: Cleansing, grounding, pain-relieving, protecting
Organs: Back, heart, muscles, nerves
Glands: None
Systems: Nervous, reproductive
Chakras: Base and Earth Star

Sodalite
Qualities: Cooling, regulating fluids, releasing, stabilizing; is excellent for mental balance
Organs: Larynx, vocal cords
Glands: Pineal, thyroid
Systems: Immune, lymphatic, metabolic
Chakras: Brow, throat

Case history: Soothing Green Calcite

Green Calcite is traditionally used to calm both nausea and anxiety. So, when a dear friend of mine had to undergo extensive chemotherapy which resulted in violent nausea, I took a large chunk into the hospital. She was particularly anxious to be home, as she felt she could get better rest and nutrition there. She curled up around the stone and instantly became calmer. It didn't totally alleviate the nausea, but it did release her anxiety about the whole process. She saw it as part of her detoxification and found great comfort in hugging her lumpy green friend. Within a couple of days she was well enough to go home.

Dealing with pain

Pain is a signal that something is out of balance in your body. It results from an excess of energy, a blockage or debility, as well as injury or insult to the body. A cool and calming crystal such as Lapis Lazuli or Rose Quartz sedates energy, whereas a stimulating one such as Carnelian or Red Jasper brings about a fast release but can instigate a healing challenge. In a healing challenge, symptoms may be exacerbated before they get better. If a crystal brings about too violent a challenge, Smoky Quartz calms the situation down.

Cathedral Quartz is excellent for pain relief, no matter what the cause. Lapis Lazuli quickly draws off a migraine, especially if this has a psychic cause (in which case place the crystal over your third eye). But you need to know where a headache stems from before you can ease it. If it is caused by stress, Amber, Amethyst or Turquoise placed on the brow or back of the neck relieves it. If it is food related, as many headaches are, a stone which calms the stomach, such as Citrine, Green Calcite or Moonstone, is appropriate.

Pain-release crystals
Amber, Amethyst, Anandalite™, Azurite with Malachite, Blue Euclase, Cathedral Quartz, Champagne Aura Quartz, Dendritic Agate, Eye of the Storm, Kutnohorite, Lapis Lazuli, Malachite, Rhodozite, Rose Quartz, Turquoise, Wind Fossil Agate

Eye of the Storm (Judy's Jasper)
Vibration: Earthy and high

Organs: Bile duct, heart, kidneys

Eye of the Storm acts as a haven during upheavals, enabling you to remain calmly centred. It draws off toxicity, rebalances the cells and stimulates the immune system. This stone sustains you during serious illness and regulates pain. It encourages the growth of healthy cells via etheric DNA. A stress-reliever, it switches off the 'fight or flight' response. It is also a life-support system for the planet during Earth healing.

The immune system

Your immune system is what keeps you healthy. It fights off bacterial and viral infections and regulates the detoxification processes in your body. In addition to the physical immune system, you have a subtle, psychic system that interacts with crystal energy. When this is active and balanced, wellbeing ensues.

One of the major governing points of the immune system is the thymus gland, which is situated in the middle of the upper chest, about a hand's breadth below the throat. (This point is also the higher heart chakra.)

Exercise: Stimulating the immune system

Bloodstone has long been used to stimulate the physical and subtle immune systems. Quantum Quattro is a more recent discovery that heals through the synergy of several minerals. Both are effective immune stimulators, but you could also use Que Sera for this exercise.

❖ With a cleansed and dedicated Bloodstone, Quantum Quattro or Que Sera, tap gently over your thymus gland (at the centre of your upper chest although either side of the breastbone may be more comfortable) for five minutes or tape the stone in place and leave it there for several hours.

Crystals for the immune system

Bloodstone

Vibration: Earthy

One of the first healing stones used by humanity, Bloodstone is associated with the blood and kidneys. In crystal healing it detoxifies the liver, improves the circulation, purifies the lymph, stimulates the production of T-cells and strengthens the immune system. It also sedates systems that are overactive but stimulates those that are under-active. It reduces mental confusion, imparts alertness and relieves chronic conditions.

Quantum Quattro

Vibration: High

A master healer, synergistic Quantum Quattro brings the body back into balance. A combination of Dioptase, Malachite, Shattuckite and Chrysocolla on Smoky Quartz, it has a dramatic effect on the human energy field. Physically, it strengthens the immune system and DNA. Protective, absorbing toxic energies, it clears psychic attack. Placed on an area of imbalance, environmental or physical, it restores equilibrium. If one Smoky Quartz is placed on the third eye and another on the solar plexus, mind, body and emotions are balanced. It heals the effects of grief, draws out deep feelings and psychosomatic causes of dis-ease and breaks unwanted ties and outworn patterns. A strong mental cleanser, it supports a positive attitude to life.

Crystal essences

Crystal essences are a gentle way to use the healing properties of stones, as the vibrations are transferred to water. Essences can be taken as drops, spritzed into the aura, rubbed on the skin or added to bathwater.

Use only cleansed, non-toxic crystals. For toxic or layered crystals, use the indirect method (*see below*).

Caution: Toxic

The following crystals may contain traces of toxic minerals. Use polished/tumbled stones, make crystal essences by the indirect method and wash your hands after handling them:

Actinolite, Adamite, Andaluscite, Ajoite, Alexandrite, Almandine Garnet, Amazonite, Aquamarine, Aragonite, Atacamite, Aurichalcite, Axinite, Azurite, Beryl, Beryllium, Bixbite, Black Tourmaline, Boji Stones, Bornite, Brazillianite, Brochantite, Bumble Bee Jasper, Cavansite, Cassiterite, Celestite, Cerrusite, Cervanite, Chalchantite, Chalcopyrite (Peacock Ore), Chryolite, Chrysoberyl, Chrysocolla, Cinnabar, Conichalcite, Copper, Covellite, Crocoite, Cryolite, Cuprite, Diopside, Dioptase, Dumortierite, Emerald, Epidote, Garnet, Gem Silica, Galena, Garnierite (Falcondoite), Goshenite, Heliodor, Hessonite Garnet, Hiddenite, Jadeite, Iolite, Klinoptilolith, Kunzite, Kyanite, Lapis Lazuli, Lazurite, Labradorite, Lepidolite, Magnetite, Malachite, Marcasite, Mohawkite, Moldavite, Moonstone,

Moqui Balls, Morganite, Orpiment, Pargasite, Pietersite, Prehnite, Psiomelane, Pyrite, Pyromorphite, Quantum Quattro, Realgar, Renierite, Rhodolite Garnet, Ruby, Sapphire, Serpentine, Spessartine Garnet, Smithsonite, Sodalite, Spinel, Spodumene, Staurolite, Stibnite, Stilbite, Sugilite, Sulphur, Sunstone, Tanzanite, Tiffany Stone, Tigers Eye, Topaz, Torbenite, Tourmaline, Tremolite, Turquoise, Uvarovite Garnet, Valentinite, Vanadinite, Variscite, Vesuvianite, Wavellite, Wulfenite, Zircon, Zoisite

Exercise: Making a crystal essence

❖ Place a crystal in spring water in a glass or crystal bowl. For toxic or delicate crystals (*see above*), use the indirect method: place the crystal in a small glass bowl and then place this in the water so that there is no direct contact between the crystal and the water.

❖ Place the bowl in the sun for several hours or overnight in moonlight if appropriate.

❖ Remove the crystal and add the activated water to two-thirds as much again brandy, vodka or white rum to preserve it. Bottle, label and store in a cool place. This is the mother tincture.

❖ To make a dosage bottle, add 7 drops of the mother tincture to a small dropper bottle filled with one-third brandy, vodka or white rum to two-thirds spring water, or fill a small spray bottle with spring water plus 7 drops of tincture.

❖ Take 7 drops of the essence three times a day, rub it onto the inside of the wrist, over the site of dis-ease or the corresponding chakra, or spritz it around your aura or your environment.

Klinoptilolith

Organs: Digestive tract, kidneys, liver

Systems: Immune, metabolic

Caution: Toxic – use with care (*see above*)

Klinoptilolith is a type of zeolite from which a pharmaceutical chemotherapy drug is made. Anti-fungal, it stimulates detoxification processes and enhances cell regulation and the body's self-healing mechanism. Research suggests that the stone moves heavy metals and free radicals out of the body, improving the brain, memory and motor function. Balancing homoeostasis and encouraging oxygenation of the cells, it absorbs electromagnetic microbes, pollutants, radioactivity and other forces that disrupt cell function. As a detoxifier, it has been shown to regenerate the lining of the gastric system and to support T-cells and the body's natural immune system. Reputedly, it supplies the metabolic system with the minerals required for optimum functioning.

Exercise: Making Shungite water

Research has shown that Shungite water has powerful antibacterial and antiviral properties. As it takes longer to become active, it is made in a different way from an essence.

✦ Immerse about 10 grams (¼ oz) of Shungite in 1 litre (1¾ pints) of water for at least 48 hours to therapeutically activate the water. You can also place the Shungite in a mesh bag in the bottom of a filter jug and continuously top up the water as it's used.

✦ Cleanse the crystals frequently.

✦ Drink several glasses a day for maximum effect.

Case history: Shungite

Under EU regulations I am not allowed to claim healing properties for crystals, but I can share anecdotal evidence with you. Three years ago, shortly after starting to drink a litre (1¾ pints) of Shungite water a day, I caught a chest infection, so I upped my intake to 2 litres (3½ pints). In the past I had been hospitalized with pneumonia due to such infections. This time, although the infection lingered a while, it did not progress to pneumonia. Since then I have drunk Shungite water every day and have had two winters completely free of coughs and colds, despite travelling on trains and planes where infection has been rife.

Crystals grids for health and wellbeing

Gridding is the art of placing stones to create an energetic net to purify, heal and energize the body. Grids are a great way to enfold yourself within crystal energies and harness their power. They encourage relaxation and induce a sense of wellbeing, as they rebalance your subtle energies and re-energize your body.

The crystals are placed around your body, so you may like to enlist the assistance of a friend, although you can lay out your own grids. Tumbled stones are perfect for grids, but points and other shapes can also be used. Join the crystals with a wand or long-pointed crystal to set the grid, or, if you are working alone, use the power of your mind.

All of the following grid shapes can be used for environmental healing (*see page 171*) and protection.

Exercise: Laying out a grid: The Star of David

The Star of David is a traditional protection layout but also creates a perfect cleansing and re-energizing grid.

You need:

- 6 cleansed and activated crystals (3 detoxing and 3 invigorating)

- a crystal wand

❖ Lie down comfortably where you will not be disturbed for 15 minutes.

❖ Place a Smoky Quartz or other detoxifying crystal below your feet, point facing down if it has one.

❖ Spread your arms out and place a Smoky Quartz or other detoxifying crystal at the end of your fingertips, point facing out if it has one.

❖ Join up the triangle with a wand or your mind and lie in it for five minutes. As you breathe out, feel any tension, stress or toxicity draining away from your body and being absorbed and transmuted by the crystal at your feet.

❖ Place a Clear Quartz, Quantum Quattro, Que Sera or other invigorating crystal above your head, point facing down if it has one.

✦ Place two more crystals just below your knees (points facing in) level with the crystals at your fingertips.

✦ Join up the triangle with a wand or your mind and lie in the Star of David for up to 15 minutes. Feel purifying and invigorating healing light coming in through the crystal above your head and filling your whole body.

✦ When you're ready, collect up the Clear Quartz (or other invigorating) crystals and then the Smoky Quartz (or other detoxifying) crystals.

✦ Stand up and connect to the Earth beneath your feet through your Earth Star to ground yourself.

Exercise: Laying out a grid: The five-pointed star

The five-pointed star is a useful protection layout but it also calls in universal love and healing to enhance your energy. If your crystals have points, lay them pointing towards the next crystal in the layout to channel the energy.

You need:

– cleansed and activated energizing or revitalizing stones

– a crystal wand

- ❖ Lie down comfortably where you will not be disturbed for 15 minutes, with your legs and arms stretched out sideways so that your body forms a five-pointed star.

- ❖ Lay a crystal above your head (if it has a point, face it towards your left foot).

- ❖ Lay a crystal below your left foot (if it has a point, face it towards your right hand).

- ❖ Lay a crystal at the end of your right hand (if it has a point, face it towards your left hand).

- ❖ Lay a crystal at the end of your left hand (if it has a point, face it towards your right foot).

- ❖ Lay a crystal below your right foot (if it has a point, face it towards your head).

- ❖ Using a crystal wand or the power of your mind and, starting with the crystal above your head, join the crystals to form the star, remembering to complete the circuit from your right foot to your head at the end.

- ❖ Lie in the star for up to 15 minutes. Breathe gently and absorb the crystal energies.

- ❖ When you are ready, pick up the crystals in the reverse order from that in which you laid them down.

- ❖ Stand up and make contact with the Earth through the Earth Star chakra beneath your feet.

Exercise: Laying out a grid: A figure of eight

The figure of eight melds high-vibration energy with Earth energy drawn up from the feet to create perfect balance. This grid is useful if you have raised your vibrations without grounding them, resulting in headaches and bodily discomfort. The grid settles the new vibrations into your physical and subtle bodies.

You need

– 5 cleansed and activated high-vibration stones

– 5 cleansed and activated grounding stones

❖   Lie down comfortably where you will not be disturbed for 15 minutes.

❖   Starting on your left-hand side at your waist, place five high-vibration stones equally spaced above the waist to the crown and down to the right-hand side.

❖   Starting on your right-hand side, place five grounding stones below your waist down to your feet and up the other side. (You can sit up to do this and then lie back down again.)

❖   Join up the stones with a wand or your mind. Remember to complete the circuit back to the first stone placed.

Gridding Crystals

✦ **Grounding and detoxifying:** Black Tourmaline, Boji Stones, Bronzite, Mahogany Obsidian, Orange River Quartz, Quantum Quattro, Que Sera, Shungite, Smoky Elestial, Smoky Quartz, Tantalite

✦ **Re-energizing and revitalizing:** Carnelian, Citrine, Golden Healer, Quantum Quattro, Que Sera, Red Jasper, Trummer Jasper

✦ **High vibration:** Anandalite™, Azeztulite, Brandenberg Amethyst, Golden Healer, Ocean Jasper; Petalite, Quartzes such as Nirvana, Rainbow Mayanite, Satyaloka, Satyamani, Selenite

SUMMARY ✍

✦ One of the most common uses for crystals is in healing.

✦ Crystals holistically balance mind, body and spirit.

✦ Crystals focus and direct energy to a specific point on the body or to an emotional or mental blockage.

✦ All illnesses ultimately stem from imbalances, blocked feelings, suppressed emotions and negative thinking.

✦ In crystal healing, crystals are placed over chakras or directly over organs, or laid out around the body to create a healing grid.

Chapter 11
Holistic healing: Emotions and psychosomatics

We all carry emotional baggage from the past: disappointments, losses and hurts. And we hold on to toxic emotions long after it would have been sensible to release them. This makes it difficult to adjust to life changes and creates psychosomatic dis-ease in which the 'illness' reflects the cause – heartbreak leads to heart attacks, rigidity to hardened arteries or joints, and so on. The cause lies deep in the subconscious mind, but psychosomatic illness is not 'imagination', it is underlying dis-ease presented in a symbolic fashion.

Crystals gently dissolve baggage such as unresolved grief, heartbreak, jealousy, anger, and so on, even when these have been carried over from a previous life. They then support positive, life-affirming emotions and bring more love into our heart.

Negative emotions and the chakras
Negative emotions are held in the chakras and subtle emotional body (*see Chapter 9*) and have a profound

effect on our organs and wellbeing. Placing crystals on the corresponding chakra for 5 to 15 minutes transmutes negative emotions into positive ones and enhances our capacity for joy. (If the negative emotion is deeply ingrained, tape the crystal in place or repeat the exercise once daily for a week or more.)

Negative quality	Chakra	Positive quality	Crystal
Powerlessness	Earth Star	Empowerment	Sceptre
Insecurity	Base	Security	Green Jade
Low self-esteem	Sacral	Self-confidence	Cat's Eye
Inferiority	Solar plexus	Empathy	Malachite
Jealousy	Heart	Compassion	Rose Quartz
Neediness	Heart	Unconditional love	Danburite
Self-delusion	Brow	Emotional clarity	Amethyst
Possessiveness	Past life	Openness	Dumortierite
Fear	Past life	Trust	Sodalite
Arrogance	Crown	Joy	Covellite

The solar plexus chakra

Location: Slightly above the waist

The sphere of emotional communication and assimilation. Blockages here lead to taking on other people's feelings and problems or being overwhelmed by your own emotions. This affects energy assimilation and utilization and mental concentration. As already mentioned, emotional 'hooks' from other people are found here too. 'Illness as theatre' can occur – playing out the emotional story through physical dis-ease.

Positive qualities: Emotional stability
Negative qualities: Inferiority and clinginess

Typical dis-eases: These are emotional and demanding – chronic anxiety, digestive problems, eating disorders and phobias, eczema and other skin conditions, 'fight or flight' adrenaline imbalances, gallstones, insomnia, ME, pancreatic failure, stomach ulcers

The heart chakra

Location: Over the heart
The sphere of love and nurturing. If it is blocked, love cannot flourish, feelings such as jealousy are common and there is enormous resistance to change.

Positive qualities: Compassion and peaceful harmony
Negative quality: Possessiveness
Typical dis-eases: These are psychosomatic and reactive – angina, asthma, chest infections, frozen shoulder, heart attacks, ulcers

Past-life chakras

Location: The bony ridge behind the ears
Three fingers' width behind your ears and continuing down to the hollow in the back of your skull lie the past-life chakras. The sphere of memory and hereditary issues, as the name suggests, these chakras hold your past-life memories, especially those of traumatic events such as violent death or emotional dis-ease. When these chakras are stimulated, intentionally or otherwise, past-life memories may shoot to the surface.

Imbalances in these chakras mean that you are stuck in the past, cannot move forward and may well be repeating your own past-life patterns or the ancestral patterns that have passed down through your family. This is also a point where people from the past can attach themselves to you and control you.

Positive qualities: Wisdom skills, instinctive knowing

Negative qualities: Emotional baggage and unfinished business. If the chakras are blown, you can be subconsciously overwhelmed by past-life trauma or irrational fears. (A typical example of this type of fear is: 'For years, I wouldn't go into woods at night in case *cavaliers* were there. I remember once standing looking at a dark wood and saying to myself, "For God's sake, this is 1984. There *won't* be any cavaliers there!" But I still didn't go in.')

Typical dis-eases: These are symbolic of the past-life condition or attitude, or may be a direct carry-over, a karmic imprint or repetition of an old injury.

Exercise: Emotional cleansing

Choose a crystal which feels right to you and ask it to clear any issues, whether you consciously recognize them or not. Malachite is particularly useful for clearing negative emotions, but other crystals will be needed to heal the site.

❖ Lie comfortably where you won't be disturbed for a while.

❖ Place a Smoky Quartz (point facing down if it has one) at your feet to absorb and transmute the emotional baggage you release.

❖ Place your selected crystal over your solar plexus or other appropriate chakra and ask that it dissolves your emotional baggage and that the Smoky Quartz absorbs the remnants.

❖ Consciously push the energy you release down your body and out of your feet into the Smoky Quartz for transmutation.

❖ If you feel an unexplained ache, tugging or pain anywhere in your body, place a Smoky Quartz crystal over it and ask that it be released and transmuted. Your intuition may give you a glimpse into the underlying cause(s), but if not, just let the feeling dissolve without needing to know why it arose.

❖ Place Danburite, Rose Quartz, Selenite or another crystal of unconditional love over your heart to pour love into all the places where you have released your baggage, gently healing them and filling them with light and love.

❖ Lie quietly until you feel lighter. If you become aware of tension in any part of your body where you are holding old emotions, place the crystal over the site and allow it to dissolve the tension.

❖ Tell yourself that when you stand up you will have let go of the past and moved into whatever the present holds. Ensure that your Earth Star chakra is open.

❖ Thank the crystals for their work and cleanse them when it is complete.

Crystals for your emotions

❖ **Amethyst** balances out emotional highs and lows, encouraging emotional centring. It gently dissolves emotional blocks.

❖ **Bloodstone** teaches you to recognize when it would be beneficial to undertake a strategic withdrawal. Encouraging you to live in the present moment, it helps you to move away from the past and highlights the effect that your expectations and previous experience have had on your emotional stability. It reduces irritability, impatience and aggressiveness and promotes selflessness.

- **Larvikite** helps you to deal flexibly with life by encouraging you not to dwell on problems. Supporting emotional healing, it goes deep into your being to release the causes of dis-ease. For assistance in seeing behind the façade people present and in knowing the true desires and agendas of both others and yourself, keep the stone in your pocket.

- **Malachite** is a very powerful emotional detoxifier, but it can bring on a catharsis that may need calming with Haematite or Smoky Quartz.

- **Mount Shasta Opal** infuses love into the emotional body and the mind to create a calm, quiet inner space. Useful for emotional healing at any level, it disperses stress. Placed at the throat, it helps you to communicate clearly and with focused intent. It is a stone of faithfulness and loyalty.

- **Porphyrite** assists in dealing with ancestral issues passed down the family line, especially involving family secrets and lies. The energetic matrix that supports the false façade is dismantled so that the truth emerges and healing, forgiveness and reconciliation can take place. It also lifts depression by deconstructing negative emotional or belief patterns and 'heavy' energies that weigh on the soul. It is excellent for karmic emotional healing, as it works without you needing to know the cause.

- **Rose Quartz** draws more love into your life. It gently dissolves old heartbreak, resentment and jealousy and releases them so that joy heals the heart.

✦ **Rosophia** dissolves self-doubt and a negative self-image. De-energizing old wounds and destructive beliefs, it offers deep compassion for all you have been through on your soul's journey and enables you to love yourself.

✦ **Smoky Quartz** stabilizes emotions during emotional trauma or stress and dissolves negative emotions, facilitating emotional detoxification. It assists in tolerating difficult times with equanimity, relieves fear and induces emotional calm.

SUMMARY 🖎

✦ Many illnesses are actually dis-eases, forms of disharmony that result from emotional baggage, ingrained beliefs, toxic emotions and holding on to old pain.

✦ Attitudes and ingrained patterns also create dis-ease, and there can be past-life causes as well. Emotions have their own vibration, which easily slip out of sync.

✦ Psychosomatic illness is not 'imagination', it is underlying dis-ease presented in a symbolic fashion.

✦ Crystals gently return the emotions to a positive pattern.

Chapter 12
Holistic healing:
Psyche and mind

Our state of mind has considerable influence on our wellbeing and physical health. Keeping our mind clear allows us to focus our thoughts and detach from any undue influences. Crystals promote clarity, concentration, focus and creativity and dissolve psychological dis-ease. They facilitate mental healing by helping us to drop into a theta brainwave state. Theta brainwaves induce a deep state of relaxation in which the subconscious mind and psychic immune system can be accessed. A theta wave state helps the body return to equilibrium and so can be utilized for profound healing, particularly as it interacts with the bioscalar waves naturally created by crystals.

Crystals can also bring profound peace of mind. There are crystals such as Auralite 23 and Rhomboid Selenite that switch off the mind – instantly. There are others, like Fluorite, that facilitate total focus and clarity. Yet others offer fresh insights and the ability to think outside the box and find creative solutions. Simply place the appropriate crystal over a mind chakra (*see below*) and allow it to do its work.

Crystal relaxation

Regular relaxation is of enormous benefit to wellbeing, and crystals can be really useful in achieving the relaxed but focused state that is particularly conducive to meditation, journeying and vision work.

Crystals for relaxation

✦ **Amethyst:** A natural tranquillizer that induces a profound sense of peace and relaxation and shuts off mind chatter.

✦ **Auralite 23:** Instantly shuts off mind chatter and induces a profound sense of relaxation.

✦ **Blue Lace Agate:** Its serene energies induce profound peace of mind and link you to higher guidance.

✦ **Green Aventurine:** Imparts a sense of wellbeing and emotional serenity.

✦ **Rhomboid Blue Selenite:** Instantly shuts off mind chatter and opens the third eye.

✦ **Smoky Quartz:** Instils a deep sense of relaxation into the physical and mental body.

Exercise: Crystal relaxation layout

✦ Lie down and make yourself comfortable. Ensure you won't be disturbed for at least 15 minutes.

✦ Place Smoky Quartz at your feet and focus on your intention to relax.

✦ Place Yellow Jasper over your solar plexus.

✦ Place Rose Quartz over your heart.

✦ Place Blue Lace Agate at your throat.

✦ Place Amethyst on your forehead.

✦ Place Clear Quartz above your head.

✦ Close your eyes, breathe gently and leave the crystals in place for 15 minutes.

✦ Remove the crystals, starting with the top of your head. When you get to your feet, be aware of the grounding cord going from your feet deep into the Earth.

Alternatively:

✦ Place a piece of Auralite 23 on either side of your head level with your ears and Bytownite (Yellow Labradorite) or Rhomboid Selenite over your third eye. You will experience instant relaxation.

Clarity of mind

Mental clarity starts with clearing your mind of extraneous thoughts. Here again, crystals can help.

Crystals for clearing the mind

✦ **Auralite 23** switches off the chattering mind, instilling laser-sharp clarity and peace.

✦ **Bloodstone** is an excellent tonic. It clears mental overload, reduces confusion and imparts alertness and stability.

Strengthening the ability to focus on solutions, it enables the mindset to adapt to changing circumstances.

- **Blue Lace Agate** facilitates self-expression, counteracts mental stress and encourages the mind to expand.

- **Carnelian** encourages analytic abilities and sharpens perception. Attuning daydreamers to everyday reality, it unites logic and intuition.

- **Clear Quartz** amplifies thought power, unlocks memory and brings about positive solutions.

- **Green Aventurine** stimulates creativity and helps you to see alternate possibilities.

- **Jasper** helps you to get to grips with problems assertively. Combining organizational abilities with imagination, it brings hidden problems to light and helps with finding new coping strategies.

- **Labradorite** balances the rational mind with intuitive wisdom.

- **Rhomboid Blue Selenite** creates a state of 'no mind' by switching off mind chatter and opening the intuition to bring in higher guidance.

- **Rose Quartz** calms the mind and induces clarity.

- **Smoky Quartz** encourages pragmatic, positive thought and the application of common sense and clear insight to problems.

- **Sodalite** dispels confusion, clarifies perceptions and releases bondage to specific ideas, encouraging the assimilation of new information. It is helpful for dyslexia and dyspraxia, as are Black Moonstone and Sugilite.

✦ **Yellow Labradorite (Bytownite)** switches off the conscious mind and opens the intuitive mind.

Exercise: Clearing and focusing the mind

A simple layout removes the racing thoughts and overactivity and clears the way for sharply focused thinking.

You need:

– 5 cleansed and activated mind-clearing crystals from the list above

– 5 of the following: Anandalite™, Auralite 23, Brandenberg Amethyst, Fluorite, Phenacite, Rhomboid Blue Selenite or other mental focus crystals

– 1 Blue Lace Agate or Septarian (optional)

✦ Lie down comfortably and ensure that you won't be disturbed for a while.

✦ Place a mind crystal above your head (point facing down if it has one). Place two crystals either side of the base of your ears.

✦ Place two more crystals, one each side, equidistant between the ear crystals and the crown crystal.

✦ Close your eyes and lie still for five minutes (extend this period if you wish). Feel the crystal energy filling your mind and quietly switching it off.

✦ If you have any thoughts, don't focus on them. Let them pass by.

✦ After five minutes, or when your mind is clear, add two Amethysts, Anandalites™, Brandenberg Amethysts, Phenacites or other mental focus crystals just below your ears, pointing up to the top of your head. This gives you instant clarity, so set out your problem and wait quietly for the answer to float into your mind.

❖ If you need to express your thoughts afterwards, add a Blue Lace Agate or Septarian crystal at your throat and keep it there.

❖ Sit up and gather your crystals together.

Fluorite

Vibration: Mid to high, depending on the type

A protective crystal, especially on the psychic and psychological levels. Enhances orderly thought, mental clarity, creativity and clear communication. Clears undue mental influence. Aids physical and mental coordination. Heightens intuition. Protects against computer and electromagnetic stress.

Chakras for clearing the mind

The throat chakra

Location: The centre of the throat

The sphere of communication. If it is blocked, thoughts and feelings can't be verbalized and truth can't be expressed. Other people's opinions cause difficulties.

Positive quality: Truthful self-expression

Negative quality: Mendacity

Typical dis-eases: are active and block communication: ADHD autism, colds and viral infections, high blood pressure, inflammation of the trachea, jaw pain and gum disease, psychosomatic dis-eases such as irritable bowel syndrome, sinus problems, sore throat/quinsy, speech impediments, thyroid imbalances, tinnitus and ear infections, tooth problems (which relate to root beliefs)

The brow chakra (third eye)

Location: Above and between the eyebrows

The sphere of intuition and mental connection. Imbalances here create a sense of being bombarded by other people's thoughts, or wild and irrational intuitions that have no basis in truth. Controlling or coercing mental 'hooks' from other people lock in and affect your thoughts.

Positive quality: Intuitive insight
Negative quality: Delusion
Typical dis-eases: these are metaphysical – autism, cataracts, iritis and other eye problems, epilepsy, high blood pressure, 'irritations' of all kinds, mental overwhelm, migraines, schizophrenia, sinus and ear infections, spinal and neurological disorders

The crown chakra

Location: The top of the head

The sphere of spiritual communication and awareness. If it is blocked, attempting to control others is common, and if it is blown, obsession and openness to spirit interference or possession can result. If it is not functioning well, excess environmental sensitivity and delusions or dementia can result.

Positive quality: Spirituality
Negative quality: Arrogance
Typical dis-eases: these arise out of disconnection – dementia, depression, electromagnetic and environmental sensitivity, insomnia or excessive sleepiness, ME, metabolic syndrome, nervous system disturbances, vague 'unwellness', also biological clock disturbances such as jet lag

Releasing patterns of the past

In addition to the chakras, the aura, the subtle electromagnetic bodies surrounding the physical body, holds embedded patterns from the past. It may have thought forms attached that are influencing us or it may be holding a soul intention that no longer serves us – one from another life or one that was put in place before incarnation but is now outdated or impossible to perform.

Undue mental influence, outdated concepts and mental imperatives all prevent us from thinking for ourselves or block a shift in consciousness. Some of these concepts may well once have been positive but have become fixed in our mind, even though they are past their sell-by date. Others may have been set up in childhood, or in previous lives. Crystals help us to release them gently and simply allow the process to unfold. Once they are cleared, we literally think – and feel – for ourselves.

Our aura may also have spirits attached that are seeking to have specific experiences through us or to control us. Clearing these calls for an experienced healer, but in an emergency, crystals can be used to detach spirits and send them to the light.

Undue mental influence

Some causes of psychological or mental dis-ease arise from outside us. There may be people around who feel that they know what is best for us, or what we *should* do. Their influence may be overt or subtle, but nonetheless powerful. They may be well-meaning, but their intent may nevertheless be manipulative and toxic. They may also have strong beliefs about us and we may pick up their thoughts and act on them, while remaining unaware of the source. In addition, strong mental conditioning may have been instilled in us when we were a child and might still be running our life, though it is now inappropriate for us.

Fortunately crystals such as Fluorite, Kunzite and Selenite help to dispel undue mental influence, as do Auralite 23 and other high-vibration Amethysts. Wear one constantly to protect yourself against invasion by other people's thoughts or beliefs.

Mental constructs and imperatives

The majority of psychological dis-ease, however, arises from within our own mind, especially the beliefs that we hold at the subconscious level – beliefs that may clash with what we think we believe. Crystals can help us dissolve all these old patterns and attachments.

Exercise: Dissolving old patterns

❖ Stand with your feet slightly apart and 'comb' all around your body, back and front, at about a hand's breadth or slightly beyond it, with a piece of Anandalite™ or Flint or a Gold or Silver Healer. If a spot feels 'sticky' or painful, rest the crystal there for a few moments. Spiral it out to release the energy.

❖ Pay special attention to the past-life chakras behind the ears and along the bony ridge at the base of the skull.

❖ Lie down comfortably and ensure you will not be disturbed.

- Place a crystal over your third eye (an Anandalite™, Auralite 23 or Brandenberg Amethyst is appropriate). If you intuitively feel that past-life issues need clearing, place an appropriate crystal such as Dumortierite or Flint either side of your ears or in the hollow at the base of your skull.

- Ask that the crystal dissolves any thoughts, vows, beliefs, imperatives, undue mental influences and so on that no longer serve you. Remind yourself that you don't need to know what these are, you are simply willing to release them right now.

- Ask that the crystal dissolves any soul contracts that are no longer relevant to your spiritual growth and any outdated soul intentions for the present lifetime. Let them go with love and forgiveness. Again, you don't need to know what they are. Simply be willing to relinquish them right now.

- Then step into the karma of grace, letting go of the past and being ready to move into whatever the present holds.

- When the process is complete, remove the crystals and thank them for their work.

Crystals for tie-cutting and spirit detachment

If you feel that someone has undue influence over your mind, you can use a crystal to cut that tie and detach yourself from them. If it is a spirit influencing you, spirit release is a specialized subject (see www.spiritrelease.org), but in an emergency a crystal can assist you in detaching an unwanted spirit hitchhiker from your aura.

In both cases, choose a crystal from the list below and 'comb' your aura with it. Essences such as Astral Clear,

Petaltone Zl4, Plant Ally and Special 8 on the crystal (*see Resources*) will assist the process.

✦ **Jasper knives** instantly cut through ties and remove hitchhikers. Dissolving old patterns, they help the etheric blueprint form a more appropriate configuration. (*They are available on request from www.angeladditions. co.uk*)

✦ **Nirvana Quartz** reminds us that spirit attachment is one situation where informed consent is not mandatory, as the soul rarely chooses to have a spirit attach. Additional stones such as Black Tourmaline, Polychrome Jasper or Tantalite may be needed to seal the aura against re-invasion.

✦ **Rainbow Mayanite** is the finest tool there is for working in the subtle etheric layers to remove ties and attachments, but it should only be used by an experienced crystal healer. It blends particularly well with Petaltone, Plant Ally and Special 8 essences. Gold and Silver Healers are the gentler version of this powerful stone and more suitable for beginners.

✦ **Stibnite** creates an energetic shield around the physical body. It separates out the pure from the dross and is an efficient tool for releasing spiritual hitchhikers or negative energy. Eliminating tentacles from clingy relationships, it also assists in tie-cutting rituals and past-life release.

SUMMARY ✍

- ❖ Your state of mind has considerable influence on your wellbeing and physical health.

- ❖ Crystals promote clarity, concentration, focus and creativity and dissolve psychological dis-ease.

- ❖ Keeping your mind clear allows you to focus your thoughts and detach from any undue influence there might be.

- ❖ Crystals facilitate mental healing by helping you to drop into a theta brainwave state.

Chapter 13
Personal protection and energy enhancement

We are all surrounded by unseen vibrations, imperceptible emanations and subtle energy fields, including thoughts and feelings, imprints and impressions that can subtly disturb our sense of wellbeing. This toxic energy is an intrusion which is silent, invisible and yet very powerful in its draining effect. A filter is needed. Crystals can help us to protect ourselves from this invisible invasion and enhance our own energy.

Self-protection

Self-protection isn't aggressive or threatening, but is simply about feeling secure within your own self. It is about creating a safe space in which to live, work and have your being. It creates healthy boundaries and a calm, quiet centre in which to simply *be*. It's about having positive emotions and constructive thoughts that create a benevolent world. It isn't really about *doing*, more about creating a tranquil space in which others cannot disturb your equilibrium –

either deliberately or by what they think or feel spilling out into the atmosphere around you.

Crystals have been used for this purpose for thousands of years, as have crystal essences. A crystal creates an interface through which you can be aware of feelings and emotions and external signals, but not be overwhelmed by them.

You need crystal protection if:

◆ You work closely with other people, particularly those who are troubled or ill.

◆ People naturally gravitate to you with their troubles.

◆ You give a great deal of energy to other people.

◆ Certain people or places leave you feeling drained and tired.

◆ You are sensitive to atmospheres.

◆ You automatically take on a friend's feelings.

◆ You live with your head in the clouds.

◆ You are anxious, nervy, on edge all the time.

◆ You have invisible feelers out, testing the air around you.

◆ You feel perpetually tired, listless, hopeless.

◆ You feel invaded, somehow *not yourself*.

◆ You dwell on things, turning them over and over in your mind.

◆ Someone is showing particularly strong animosity towards you.

◆ You are a water sign: Cancer, Scorpio or Pisces.

✦ You are psychic or a healer or therapist.

The key to good protection is to find exactly the right crystal for the situations in which you find yourself. Amber, Amethyst, Black Tourmaline, Carnelian and Smoky Quartz were traditionally used for protection, particularly for turning back ill-wishing or jealousy, and are highly protective when worn around the neck, but Tantalite provides twenty-first-century protection, as does Polychrome Jasper or Shungite. Healer's Gold is a rare crystal but worth seeking out if you need to create an interface.

Crystals for shielding

Black Tourmaline

Vibration: Earthy

Deflects negative energies, protects against geopollutants, EMFs and radiation. Turns back anger, ill-wishing and attack. Increases physical vitality. Strengthens the immune system.

Tape it to a mobile phone, place it next to a computer or other source of EMF, hold it or keep it in a pocket, place it between your house and a source of radiation or EMF.

Labradorite

Vibration: High

A wonderful energy protector that also pulls in spiritual power. An excellent crystal for healers and those who work with other people, it enhances intuition whilst creating an interface that prevents other people's problems, negative thoughts or energies from being taken on.

Tantalite

Vibration: Earthy

A useful stone of protection, Tantalite soaks up negative energy and guards against psychic vampirism or environmental pollution. Blocking invasion by external forces, it creates an energetic grid around the body to 'repel boarders'. Clearing the effect of psychic attack or ill-wishing, it removes hooks, attachments, implants, mental imperatives and core beliefs lodged in the etheric or physical body from present or previous lives. It also shields the body so that nothing else attaches. It is rich in manganese, an important physiological constituent with a powerful antioxidant and metabolic function. It also assists in feeling nurtured and guided by higher beings.

Grid or wear Tantalite to deflect radiation and other adverse energies.

Amber

Vibration: Medium

The fossilized resin of ancient trees, Amber is not a crystal, but it has always been prized for its protective qualities. With strong connections with the Earth, it is a grounding stone for higher energies. A powerful healer and cleanser, it draws dis-ease from the body and aids tissue revitalization. It also cleanses the environment and the chakras, absorbing negative energies and transmuting them into positive forces that aid the body in healing itself.

Additional shielding crystals include Actinolite, Aegerine, Amber, Apache Tear, Aquamarine, Bronzite, Chlorite or Smoky Quartz, Citrine, Haematite, Marcasite, Nuummite,

Polychrome Jasper, Purpurite and Shungite.

Case history: Black Tourmaline to the rescue

My first introduction to the protective powers of Black Tourmaline came from a workshop participant many years ago. She was wearing it around her neck. She told me that she had been under severe ill-wishing from a colleague who had become jealous of her advancement. She had been almost literally on her knees, unable to stand upright because of extreme energy debilitation, and a friend had given her a piece of Black Tourmaline to stop the attack. Overnight she had recovered her energy and been able to deal constructively with the situation. Since then I have seen Black Tourmaline work in many similar situations.

Exercise: Protecting yourself

- ❖ Wear a Black Tourmaline, Labradorite or Polychrome Jasper crystal around your neck.

- ❖ For advanced protection, use Healer's Gold, or wear Tantalite placed in a spiral.

Exercise: The Amber melt

For fast protection:

- ❖ Hold an Amber crystal over your head.

- ❖ Picture the Amber melting and running down the outside of your aura, creating a crystal coating that protects you.

The psychic shield

A psychic shield protects your energy from being invaded or drawn upon by others and turns back negative energy before it reaches you. Create a shield by programming a crystal and keeping it with you constantly. If you find a shield-shaped piece, so much the better.

Exercise: The Tantalite cage

❖ Once you are attuned to Tantalite, use the power of your imagination to create a Tantalite 'cage' around your whole body.

❖ Whenever you feel the need for additional protection, mentally shout 'Tantalite!' and feel that protective cage strengthening around you.

Energy enhancement

As well as protecting your energy, you can also enhance it. Your own attitude can play a large part in this. If you are joyful and feel that life is abundant and nourishing, life flows well and good things come to you. Fear, however, pulls to you the very things of which you are afraid. Fear erodes your energy, joy enhances it. So the key to energy enhancement is to surround yourself with good vibrations and to be positive.

❖ Be in a space that feels good – if it doesn't, change this (*see Chapter 14*).

❖ Think positive thoughts and have positive expectations.

❖ Avoid fear.

❖ Keep calm in a crisis.

❖ Do the things you enjoy.

❖ Be with people who boost your energy.

❖ Wear appropriate crystals or grid them around you (*see page 121*).

The power of visualization

You can also use visualization to help you. Visualization is seeing things in your mind's eye. Closing your eyes and looking up to the point between and slightly above the centre of your eyebrows helps images to form, as does letting your eyes go out of focus when looking into a crystal. However, you don't need to *see* anything to *feel* the benefit.

Exercise: Bringing in good vibes

This crystal visualization combines the power of your mind with that of your crystals. (You may like to record this visualization or have a friend read it out to you.)

You need Quartz, Que Sera or Selenite.

❖ Sit comfortably and close your eyes. Look up to the point between and above your eyebrows.

❖ Open your palm chakras to radiate the crystal energy.

❖ Hold your crystal in whichever hand feels more comfortable.

❖ Breathe gently. Let your attention go to the top of your head, taking the hand with the crystal there. Hold the crystal as far as you can reach above your head.

❖ Imagine that someone has switched on a very bright white light above your head and this is focused through your crystal. Feel the brightness and the warmth of this light mingling with the vibrant crystal energies. It is full of good vibrations.

❖ Feel the crystal light begin to move down through your head (move your crystal downwards as you go). As it moves, the crystal light seeks out any dark place, filling it with light and joy.

❖ The crystal light moves through your skull, going through all the folds and creases of your brain, filling it with crystal light. The vibrations feel vibrant and tingly and your mind opens up and accepts them. The happiness in the crystal light expands through your whole head. Your eyes are bright, your hearing acute. Your nose and mouth fill with the crystal light as you breathe in bubbles of crystal energy.

❖ The crystal light passes on down through your throat and neck and into your shoulders, arms and hands. You feel the vibrations tingling down to your fingertips. The bubbles of crystal light pass into your lungs, energizing as they go. Your back has a column of crystal light supporting it and ribs of crystal light around it, as the crystal light moves on down through your internal organs, lighting them up as it goes.

❖ Be aware of the crystal light entering your heart, dissolving any pain or grief and filling your heart with joy and good vibrations. Feel your blood picking up the vibrations as it passes through the heart and lungs and helping to carry the crystal light to every part of your body.

❖ When the crystal light reaches your solar plexus, it pauses for a while. As you breathe, it cleanses the emotions that you hold in your solar plexus, encouraging the joyous ones and transmuting any painful ones.

✦ Then the crystal light moves on down into your hips and belly. When it reaches the base of your spine and your reproductive organs, you feel your creative energy begin to resonate in harmony with it. Let this creative force flow wherever it will.

✦ Allow the crystal light to move on down through your thighs and legs to your feet until your toes tingle.

✦ Be aware that your whole body is filled with this vibrating crystal light. Your energy is replenished. Your body is in balance, your emotions are harmonious, your thoughts positive.

✦ Curl the energy down into your dantien, a small power-generating sphere on top of your sacral chakra. Store the energy here until you need it. A deep breath or holding the crystal over this place is all that will be needed to release it when required.

✦ The crystal light is then switched off, but you remain filled with it.

✦ Take your attention down to your feet. Be very aware of the contact they make with the Earth. Feel them holding you and grounding you on the Earth and into your body.

✦ When you are ready, open your eyes.

Combating energy vampires

It is all too easy to lose energy to other people. The main symptom is a feeling of weariness or slight depression, low energy and a tugging or tweaking pain under your left armpit. The leaching occurs through the solar plexus but happens to a greater extent through the spleen chakra, which is located about a hand's breadth beneath the left armpit (*see page 156*). So, if you get a nagging pain there, an energy vampire is at work. This may be a family member, partner or friend, client or work colleague. Fortunately the antidote is simple: unhook them and protect the energy portal.

The spleen chakra

Location: Below the left armpit

The sphere of assertion and empowerment. If this chakra is imbalanced, you have anger issues or suffer constant irritation, with your body turning in to attack itself. If it is too open, other people draw on your energy, leaving you depleted, particularly at the immune level.

Typical dis-eases: these arise from depletion – anaemia, lethargy, low blood sugar

Exercise: Closing the energy portal

❖ Cleanse your spleen chakra by spiralling out a Flint, Quartz point or Rainbow Mayanite to clear any hooks or energetic connections, or use a Jasper knife (*available from www.angeladditions.co.uk on request*).

❖ Tape a Green Aventurine, Green Fluorite, Jade or Tantalite crystal over the spleen chakra, or wear one on a long chain so that it reaches to the end of your breastbone.

SUMMARY ✍

* Unseen energetic dimensions surround and interpenetrate the physical.

* Toxic energy is silent, invisible and yet very powerful in its draining effect.

* Keeping your energies high and clear gives you subtle protection from otherwise detrimental outside influences.

* Other people's thoughts and feelings can adversely affect you if you don't shield your own energies.

* Self-protection is about feeling secure within your own self.

* Crystals filter energy and create an interface with another energy field.

Chapter 14
Crystals for safe space

Crystals are an excellent way to ensure that you live and work in a good space. Houses and other spaces have a subtle energetic history. An imprint is left by everyone who lives there. Neighbours add their vibes too, as do events that have previously occurred. Crystals are the perfect tools to keep your environment energetically clean.

But safe outer space starts with secure inner space. Remember that 'like attracts like'. You cannot create a safe space for yourself if your motives, emotions and behaviour are not in harmony. Similarly, if you share space with an irritable or pessimistic person, you can't keep that energy out of your space – but you can place a crystal to absorb and transmute it.

Bear in mind too that 'as you think, so you are'. Think positively. Think clean, safe space and you'll create it.

Practical space protection

You can't protect your space from your own negativity or the negativity of anyone who shares that space with you.

You must clear it from yourself first and then from your space, which is where crystals help.

Crystals have benefits which you feel rather than see. They absorb and cleanse subtle emanations and emotional debris within your space. They are particularly effective for soaking up the electromagnetic disturbances created by televisions, computers, phones, power lines and suchlike (EMFs). A protective crystal such as Black Tourmaline, Graphic or Smoky Elestial Quartz placed by the front door protects the whole house, preventing an influx of negative vibes. Traditionally, Sardonyx placed here repels thieves. Carnelian or Citrine just inside the entrance invites in abundance and good vibes, and Selenite brings in light. If you'd like your home to be filled with love and harmony, Rose Quartz just inside the front door does the trick, while a beautiful pink or blue Aragonite sphere radiates joy, love and serenity into your home.

If the protective crystal has a point, point it away from your house to deflect negative energy and transmute it into positive. If you want to call in beneficial energies, point the crystal towards you.

How do you find the right spot? Let the crystal tell you! Or dowse for it (*see page 17*). Some places are obvious. A large piece of Rose Quartz by your bed encourages love and harmony, but may disrupt sleep if placed too close.

The crystals in the list below are equally effective for any 'bad vibes' that may be affecting your home or workplace. They are excellent for combating 'sick building syndrome' too.

Exercise: Creating a safe space

Cleansing a space

❖ To keep a room energetically clean, place a large piece of Black Tourmaline, Calcite, Graphic Smoky Quartz, Smoky Quartz or Tourmalinated Quartz in a position where it won't be disturbed and ask it to transmute negative energies.

❖ Remember to cleanse it frequently.

❖ You can also make a crystal essence to spritz around the space (*see page 119*).

Bringing in light

❖ To keep a space energetically purified and filled with spiritual light for long periods, put Petaltone Z14 on a large piece of Selenite – it works for six months and more.

Flushing away negative vibes

❖ A large Chlorite Quartz hung point down in the lavatory cistern absorbs negative energy from your house and transmutes it with each flush.

Calming noisy neighbours

❖ Place Rose Quartz near the wall you share with your noisy neighbours to radiate peace and calm them down.

❖ Remember to cleanse the crystal regularly.

Combating subtle pollutants

Most of us are bombarded with unseen EMF radiation or geopollutants (adverse energy lines and toxicity in the ground), which can have adverse effects, especially on those who are psychic or energy-sensitive, making them feel drained and ill.

Exercise: Protection against EMFs

✦ Switch on your computer or mobile phone or stand close to your television. With your hands, sense the energy field around it and feel the effect it has on your body and your energy. If it has no effect, you need go no further.

✦ If you become headachy or your energy drops or you feel any other kind of adverse reaction, place Amazonite, Black Tourmaline or Shungite between you and the EMF source. Feel the change as the emissions are blocked.

✦ Take the Amazonite, Black Tourmaline or Shungite around your body to find the best place for it. Wear it over your thymus (just above the heart) or place it over the spleen chakra under your left arm or wherever it feels it is working best.

Note: If you begin to feel tired when wearing or using Shungite, cleanse it immediately. It is sensible to have at least two pieces, one in use and one being cleansed.

Case history: Shielding the electricity sub-station

I'm all too aware of the detrimental effects of EMF emissions on my energy field. So moving to live opposite an electricity sub-station could have been bad news. I have, however, turned this around to re-energize myself with the use of crystals.

First I held the intention that the emissions would help me to heal. On moving in, I gridded the garden with pieces of Black Tourmaline, positioning one at each corner, and put these around my bed as well. I placed Amazonite, Amethyst, Herkimer Diamonds and large Smoky Quartz points on the windowsills (with the points pointing away from the house to deflect the energy). Later I added Shungite. The house feels energetically clear and, on dowsing, registers no adverse EMF emissions.

My computer is surrounded by Amazonite, Fluorite, Lepidolite and Shungite to further protect my energy.

Crystals for combating environmental pollution

- **Amazonite** and **Black Tourmaline** block radar/mobile phone mast emanations.

- A **Black Tourmaline rod in Quartz**, **Smoky Quartz** or **Tourmalinated Quartz** guards against terrorist attack or can be used to heal the effects of violence or trauma.

- **Graphic Smoky Quartz** soaks up and transmutes negative emissions, stabilizing and protecting the space around you.

- **Malachite** is particularly efficient at soaking up nuclear or Earth radiation.

- **Shungite** is the crystal *par excellence* for shielding against EMFs.

- **Smoky Quartz** is excellent for blocking electromagnetic smog of any kind.

❖ **Turquoise** is an all-round environmental healer and cleanser.

Graphic Smoky Quartz

Vibration: High

A fairly new discovery from Madagascar (available from the USA as Zebra Stone and elsewhere as Calcite Writing Stone), Graphic Smoky Quartz is a strongly purifying stone that grounds and helps you feel safe in physical incarnation. Invigorating for the body, it infuses dynamic energy and a feeling of wellbeing. The Smoky Quartz has been tightly compressed into Feldspar, and this crystal assists in feeling safe in traumatic situations, getting to the core of things and instilling trust. It opens and cleanses all the chakras and activates metaphysical abilities. A shamanic stone that enables travelling silently through the lower realms, it imparts the stealth of a big cat. Insisting on integrity in its use, it helps find a creative way to approach your goals and is excellent for strengthening the structures of the physical or subtle bodies.

Gridding for safe space

Crystal grids create and maintain safe space. The easiest way to grid a room or other space is to place a crystal in each corner, as this creates an energy grid across the whole room. However, you can grid the room with whatever pattern feels right at the time.

All stones laid in grids should be cleansed and dedicated before use, but remember to allow them to do what they do best rather than what you feel they should be doing.

Dowsing establishes the exact placement for the crystals.

Join the crystals with a wand or long-point crystal such as a Lemurian or Quartz to set the grid. If the lines of force pass through walls and solid objects, use the power of your mind or a crystal wand to connect the points. Take it up to the point on the wall, visualize it passing through the wall and then walk around to the other side to recommence the line.

Exercise: Creating a safe space grid

❖ Place small pieces of Black Tourmaline, Graphic Smoky Quartz or Shungite in each corner of a room, or your house, to keep out bad vibes and transmute negative energies.

❖ Adding raw or polished Labradorite or ethereal white Selenite will draw in light to assist in your work or your daily and spiritual life.

❖ Join the stones up with the power of your mind or a Quartz wand to create a three-dimensional energetic grid that protects your entire space.

Safe-space crystals for gridding

❖ To absorb geopathic stress: Black Tourmaline, Graphic Smoky Quartz, Labradorite, Smoky Quartz, Tantalite

❖ To cleanse negative energies: Amber, Bloodstone, Shungite

❖ To clear environmental pollution: Graphic Smoky Quartz in Feldspar, Malachite (particularly good for radioactive emissions), Turquoise

❖ To deflect psychic attack: Black Tourmaline, Labradorite, Shungite, Tantalite

- To guard against space invasion (place at the corners of the room or grid in a pentacle or Star of David, *see pages 122–23 and 172*): Black Tourmaline, Graphic Smoky or Elestials, large Quartz cluster, large Smoky Quartz points, Rose Quartz, Selenite

- To neutralize EMFs: Amazonite, Black Tourmaline, Fluorite, Shungite, Smoky Quartz

- To prevent crime (grid around the outside of the house or in the corners of the room): Kyanite, Sardonyx, Selenite

- To replace negative vibes with positive, loving vibrations: Amethyst, Rose Quartz, Selenite

Triangulation

A triangulation grid neutralizes negative energy and brings in positive. It also provides protection or healing while you sleep, so this is a useful grid to build around your bed or to create safe space.

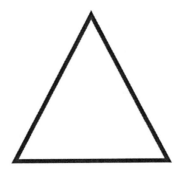

Exercise: Laying out a triangulation grid

You need:

– 3 cleansed and activated crystals

– a crystal wand

❖ Place a crystal (point facing down) above your head or at the head of your bed.

❖ Place a crystal below your left leg (stretched out sideways) or at the left-hand corner of your bed.

❖ Place a crystal below your right leg (stretched out sideways) or at the right-hand corner of your bed.

❖ Bring your legs together, join up the triangle and lie comfortably in it for 15 minutes or during the night.

You can also lay a double triangle – the Star of David – around your bed or anywhere in your space that needs protection.

The zig-zag

The zig-zag layout is particularly useful for sick building syndrome and for transmuting environmental pollution. Place appropriate crystals as shown on the diagram below. Cleanse regularly.

Things that go bump in the night

If you are troubled by restless spirits, gremlins or the impact of events that occurred in the past, a crystal is of great assistance. Quite apart from their own cleansing properties, they make great carriers for safe-space and clearing essences (*see Resources*). The synergistic effect is much stronger than using an essence or crystal alone.

Exercise: Dealing with ghosts

❖ Put a few drops of Petaltone Astral Clear on a Clear Quartz crystal.

❖ Ask the crystal to send the spirit to the light.

❖ Leave it overnight to do its work.

For slightly more troublesome spirits, Petaltone Special 8 or Z14 works well on Labradorite or Quartz as a carrier. However, serious activity requires specialist help.

SUMMARY

❖ Crystals counteract any toxic imprints or emanations from the space around you, replacing them with beneficial energies.

❖ Clear negativity from yourself first and then your space.

❖ Grids create safe space and can be left in place for long periods.

Chapter 15
Environmental healing

Just as the physical body has a chakra system, so does the Earth. And just as crystals can be used to heal areas of disturbance or blockages in a person's energetic system, so they can be used to heal the Earth.

Earth imbalances are caused by factors such as geopollutants, mining, nuclear testing, shifting of the tectonic plates of the planet during earthquakes and the energetic imprint of events that have taken place at a site. Earth healing through the chakras and other vortex points opens, purifies, aligns and heals the Earth's energy field, revitalizes its energetic matrix and maintains overall planetary wellbeing.

The Earth's chakra system

The Earth's chakra system links sacred sites around the planet. Earth chakras cover vast distances, radiating out from a central sacred site. Not everyone agrees on exactly where these chakras are. Additional Earth chakras are coming online at the moment to assimilate higher vibrational energies and over 156 have been identified over the last 20 years by Robert Coon (*for more details of his work visit www.earthchakras.org*).

The Seven Major Earth Chakras are as follows:

- **Base:** Mount Shasta, California (alternatives: Black Mesa, Sedona; the Grand Canyon)

- **Sacral:** Lake Titicaca, South America (alternatives: Amazon river; Machu Picchu)

- **Solar plexus:** Uluru, Australia

- **Heart:** Glastonbury, England (alternative: River Ganges, India)

- **Throat:** Great Pyramid, Egypt

- **Third Eye:** Mount Fuji, Japan (alternative: Kuh-e Malek Siah, Iran)

- **Crown:** Mount Kailash, Tibet

Earth healing

For Earth healing, crystals can be placed on the chakras themselves or on maps. Specific crystals work well for particular needs. Blue, brown or white Aragonites are powerful Earth healers that can be gridded around the house to keep the environment healthy and the neighbour vibes positive. They can also be placed on maps in areas where the Earth moves uneasily, to stabilize it. Atlantasite can be buried in the ground wherever there has been death and destruction on the land as it clears and restructures the Earth's energy field filling it with positive energy.

Crystals for Earth healing

Aragonite

Vibration: Earthy to high, depending on colour and type (Brown Aragonite is earthy; pink, white, lilac and blue are high to extremely high).

A grounding and healing crystal. Deepens our connection with the Earth. Combines well with Black Tourmaline (absorbs negativity, calms disturbance), Flint (stabilizes the ground) and Halite (powerfully cleansing). Brown Aragonite is particularly useful for transforming geopathic stress and blocked ley lines.

Smoky Elestial Quartz

Vibration: Exceedingly high (as with all elestials)

One of the finest transmutors of negative energy. A powerful catalyst for change. Working at multi-dimensional levels, it restructures energy fields and facilitates cellular healing. Shifts are immensely fast, but equilibrium is held. Grounds grids into everyday reality, anchors healing for the body or for the Earth. Pulls negative energy out of the environment, transmutes it and protects the whole area. Reframes the etheric blueprint and ancestral line, reprograms cellular memory and restores power to future generations. Releases karmic group enmeshment where the same patterns repeat life after life. Assists spirit release work. Grid it around a bed to block the effects of geopathic stress.

Grids for Earth Healing

As we have seen, gridding is the art of placing crystals to restore equilibrium, whether to a site or to the planet itself. When gridding for Earth healing, you don't have to visit a site, as the layout can be done on a map.

When placing crystals on a map, or at a site, dowse for the right position for the crystals or use your intuition. Remember to allow energy to flow through you and to harness the power of the crystal. Don't use your own energy. Join up the points of the grid with a wand.

The Pentangle: The five-pointed star

This powerful Earth-healer formation is particularly suitable for map work. Follow the direction of the arrows on the diagram when placing crystals and remember to go back to the start crystal to complete the circuit.

Exercise: Healing ancient trauma with the five-pointed star

Choose a site where a battle, massacre or other traumatic event took place, or where there has been significant Earth trauma, such as an earthquake or tsunami. Find a map of the site sufficiently large to place crystals on, or visit the site itself.

You need:

- 5 Aragonite or other Earth-healing stones
- 1 Smoky Elestial Quartz

❖ Dowse to find your starting point above the site (or use north) and place an Aragonite crystal on that spot.

❖ Move down to the right (as you look at the map or walk the site) and place an Aragonite below and to the side of the site.

❖ Move up and to the left and place an Aragonite above and to the side of the site.

❖ Move across and to the right and place an Aragonite to encompass the site.

❖ Move down and to the left to place the final Aragonite.

❖ Join up the five-pointed star with a wand, ensuring that you return to the first crystal laid.

❖ Place a Smoky Elestial Quartz in the centre.

❖ Ask that the trauma or energetic pollution or disturbance be transmuted and the site brought back into equilibrium.

❖ Leave the map with the crystals in place to do their healing work. Leave the crystals in place at a site.

❖ You will know the work is complete by dowsing or sensing that the crystals have ceased to send out healing energy to the site, or there may be a dramatic change in the situation. If using a map, dismantle the star and send any residual healing to the Earth. Otherwise, leave the crystals in place at the site.

Note: You can lay the same configuration over one of the Earth's chakras to help restore the Earth's energetic grid. Other Elestials, such as Amethyst, Clear or Rose Quartz bring unconditional love to an area.

SUMMARY ✍

❖ Crystals are potent tools for environmental healing. They transmute areas of disturbance or ancient trauma and repair the Earth's energetic grid.

❖ They can be placed directly onto the ground or on maps to restore equilibrium to an area.

❖ They also create sacred space.

❖ Remember to cleanse the crystals regularly.

Chapter 16
Crystal meditation and expanded awareness

Crystals are a wonderful source of strength during times of change, but where they really come into their own is in bringing about a vibrational shift of consciousness, literally taking us into a new dimension – or, rather, opening all possible dimensions.

There are many crystals available now whose stated aim is to usher in a 'new age' of unity consciousness, an integrated perception of being human and divine at the same time. But they also point out that we cannot achieve this unity until we have completed our individual healing and growth work. One way to do this is through meditation.

Crystal meditation

There are two ways of working with crystals for meditation:

1. Gazing into a crystal ball, cluster, palmstone (a polished flattish-shaped disc or oval that fits perfectly into your palm) or crystal point.

2. Laying out a meditative mandala with a handful of stones.

Exercise: Meditating with a crystal

You need:

– a crystal ball

– a cluster, point or palmstone

❖   Settle yourself comfortably where you won't be disturbed.

❖   Open your palm chakras and hold your crystal in your lap.

❖   Breathe gently, letting each out-breath be longer than the in-breath.

❖   As you breathe out, let go of any stress or tension you may feel.

❖   As you breathe in, draw the energy of the crystal up your arms to calm and centre yourself.

❖   Allow your breathing to settle into a steady rhythm.

❖   With softly focused eyes, look into your crystal.

❖   Notice its shape, its weight, its colour.

❖   Allow yourself to wander through its inner planes and landscape.

❖   When you are ready, close your eyes and remain connected to the crystal energy.

❖   When your meditation is complete, open your eyes and take two deep breaths.

❖   Put your crystal down and stand up with your feet firmly on the floor. Check that your Earth Star is open and grounding you.

Using a meditative mandala

A mandala is a sacred form or pattern. Its repeating elements calm and focus the mind. You can lay out radiating or enclosed mandalas. A simple crystal mandala can be formed by making a wheel with the spokes and rim in one type or colour of crystal and the spaces filled in with different coloured crystals, but you can use your imagination or intuition to create one for yourself. Move slowly and with focused intention as you place each stone.

Exercise: Laying out a crystal mandala

You need:

– a large tumble stone or cluster for the centre

– 6 long-point crystals for the spokes

– 18 tumble stones for the rim and 6–7 for the inner circle

– 6 types of tumble stones for infilling

– a suitable cloth

❖ Sit comfortably, or walk around a small table if you prefer a moving meditation.

❖ Breathe gently and bring your attention into yourself.

❖ Spread the cloth in front of you.

❖ Place the large tumble or cluster in the centre.

❖ Place six to seven small tumbles around it.

❖ Place six long-point crystals to form spokes out from the centre.

❖ Place 18 tumble stones to form the outer rim.

❖ Fill in each section from the centre out.

❖ Contemplate the mandala through half-closed, softly focused eyes.

❖ When your meditation is complete, gather the crystals up again.

❖ Make contact with the ground with your feet. Ensure that your Earth Star chakra is open.

Soul expansion

High-vibration crystals raise our frequency, enabling soul expansion, the opening of the higher chakras and effortless multi- and inter-dimensional journeying, especially when combined in grids. But common sense must prevail and we need to be anchored at the same time.

Crystals for higher consciousness

Anandalite™

Vibration: Exceedingly high, with a massive number of bioscalar waves

Activates psychic and physical immune systems. Purifies and aligns the whole chakra system to higher frequencies. Its natural iridescent rainbows harmonize the lightbody with the Earth vibration, preparing the central nervous system for a vibrational shift. Also deconstructs detrimental energy structures and restructures appropriately for a consciousness shift. Strips you to the bare bones of your soul and rebuilds your energy patterns to accommodate the energy shift into enlightenment on Earth. Takes you into the interconnectedness of all life for a quantum uplift. Introduces the limitless possibilities of multi-dimensional being.

Brandenberg Amethyst

Vibration: Extremely high

Holds the perfect blueprint of All That Is. Repatterns all the subtle layers and levels of being, imprinting the most perfect pattern possible. Takes you into expanded awareness of multi-dimensions.

Rainbow Mayanite

Vibration: Exceptionally high, with an immense number of bioscalar healing waves

The ultimate crystal for rainbow chakra healing and stepping onto your true path. De-energizes old patterns from any source, taking out the debris and karmic encrustations, pulls out any toxic dross absorbed from other people or the environment. Builds new supportive structures. Takes you into the depths of yourself, to how your soul is manoeuvring you onto your pathway and how an apparently detrimental situation offers you soul gifts. Offers enormous support during change.

The higher chakras

If you are a beginner, higher-chakra activation is best done slowly, one chakra at a time, until you are sure that a chakra is functioning well and you can move on to the next one. But if you have been raising your vibrations already, your higher chakras may have opened spontaneously and you may need to learn how to control them, opening and closing as appropriate.

We'll look at this in more depth later, but first, here are the higher chakras:

The Heart Seed chakra

Location: At the base of the breastbone

Function: Soul remembrance

When functioning well: A person recalls the reason for incarnation, their connection to the divine plan, the tools available to manifest potential

When blown or blocked: A person is rootless, purposeless, lost

The Higher Heart chakra

Location: Above the heart

Function: Unconditional love

When functioning well: A person is forgiving, accepting, spiritually connected

When blown or blocked: A person is spiritually disconnected, grieving, needy, a psychic vampire

The Soma chakra

Location: Above the third eye, at the hairline

Function: Spiritual connection; the place where the subtle bodies attach themselves

When functioning well: A person is spiritually aware and fully conscious

When blown or blocked: A person is cut off from spiritual nourishment and connection. When this chakra is blown it is all too easy for discarnate spirits to attach.

The Soul Star chakra

Location: Above the head

Function: Spiritual enlightenment/illumination

When functioning well: Provides ultimate soul connection, objective perspective on past

When blown or blocked: Results in spiritual arrogance, soul fragmentation, a messiah complex, rescuing not empowering; can lead to soul fragmentation, spirit attachment, ET invasion or being overwhelmed by ancestral spirits

The Stellar Gateway

Location: Above the Soul Star

Function: Cosmic doorway to other worlds

When functioning well: Provides communication with enlightened beings

When blown or blocked: Becomes a source of cosmic disinformation that leads to delusion, deception and disintegration, leaving a person unable to function in the everyday world

The Alta Major

Location: Inside the skull

A major factor in accelerating and expanding consciousness. The anchor for a multi-dimensional subtle energy body (often known as the lightbody), it unites metaphysical sight and intuitive insight. Holding valuable information about our ancestral past and the ingrained patterns that have governed human life and limited awareness, it also contains our past-life karma and the contractual agreements we made before incarnating. Activating it enables us to read our soul's plan. This chakra is a complex merkaba-like geometric shape within and around the skull that stretches from the base of the skull to the crown, connecting the past-life and soma chakras, hippocampus, hypothalamus, pineal and pituitary glands with the third eye and the higher crown chakras. Its link to the throat chakra facilitates the expression of information from higher dimensions.

Positive function: Creates a direct pathway to the supraconsciousness and intuitive mind. Brings instinctive knowledge of spiritual purpose. Reputedly the Alta Major chakra has been imprinted with 'divine codes' that, when activated, allow cosmic evolution to manifest fully on Earth.

Imbalances: these show as 'dizziness' or 'floatiness', eye problems including cataracts and floaters, feelings of confusion, headaches including migraines, loss of sense of purpose and spiritual depression.

Higher chakra crystals

Amphibole, Anandalite™, Angel's Wing Calcite, Azeztulite™, Brandenberg Amethyst, Citrine, Hungarian Quartz, Lemurian Seed, Nirvana, Phenacite, Rainbow Mayanite, Satyaloka and Satyamani Quartz, Selenite, Trigonic Quartz

Exercise: Activating the higher chakras

The activation should be carried out with the basic chakras cleansed and open (*see Sensing Blockages and Balancing the Chakras, page 103*). If you don't have the appropriate crystals, you can use the *Crystal Wisdom Oracle* cards or the images in *101 Power Crystals*.

Note: Open these chakras slowly and in order. Take your time. Don't rush the process.

❖ Place a Higher Heart chakra crystal such as Danburite, Rose Quartz or Tugtupite over the Higher Heart chakra and leave it in place for two to five minutes. This chakra can be left open.

❖ Place a Higher Heart chakra crystal such as Tugtupite over the Heart Seed chakra at the base of the breastbone and feel the influx of universal love that floods into the chakra and through your whole being. This chakra can be left open.

❖ Place a Preseli Bluestone or other cosmic anchor crystal such as Flint over the Soma chakra. Open this chakra when you want to go journeying and close it when you want to stay in your physical body.

❖ Place a high-vibration crystal such as Anandalite™, Azeztulite, Rainbow Mayanite or Selenite on the Soul Star, which connects you to your soul and highest self. Invoke your higher self to guard it well. Close the chakra (*see page 96*) when not using the portal for journeying or guidance.

❖ Before opening the Stellar Gateway, invoke your guardian angel or other protective being (*see page 221*) to guard it well while you journey or seek guidance in other realms. Place Anandalite™, Nirvana Quartz, Rainbow Mayanite, Selenite or Trigonic Quartz on the chakra to open the portal. Close the portal and the chakra when you have completed your journey.

❖ Use Anandalite™ to activate the Alta Major chakra. Place in the hollow at the base of the skull.

❖ Remember to close the chakras when the exercise is complete.

Crystal journeys

Crystals can take you far out in the universe or deep inside yourself or to the shamanic worlds. Before undertaking such journeys, however, you need to grow your shamanic and cosmic anchors to ensure that you always return to your body.

Your shamanic anchor

Before journeying, ensure that you are in a safe space by gridding with protective crystals (*see page 164*). Always open your shamanic anchor (*see page 12*) before journeying.

Shamanic anchor crystals include: Boji Stones, Elestial Smoky Quartz, Flint, Graphic Smoky Quartz, Haematite, Smoky Quartz, Stibnite.

Your cosmic anchor

A cosmic anchor helps your subtle body find its way back to your physical body. It assists in journeying safely through other dimensions and knowing your way back.

Cosmic anchor crystals include: Brandenberg Amethyst, Elestial Quartz, Flint, Preseli Bluestone, high-vibration Quartzes, Selenite, Stibnite, Tantalite.

Exercise: Growing your cosmic anchor

❖ Place your crystal on the Soma chakra (on your hairline above the third eye, above and between your eyebrows). The cosmic anchor also helps connect to your higher self, the part that is not fully in incarnation and therefore sees much further.

❖ From your Soma chakra, feel a silver cord growing outwards and upwards. This cord passes up through the higher chakras, meeting your higher self. From your higher self, the cosmic anchor passes through the outer layer of the Earth's mantle and into space. In the constellation of Sagittarius it hooks itself onto the tip of the archer's arrow, where the galactic centre is located. It keeps you balanced between Earth and cosmos, spirit and matter, and always shows you the way home to your body.

Preseli Bluestone

Vibration: Earthy and high

Healing stone of the ancestors. Grounds and focuses. Ideal for journeying, as there is an inbuilt sense of direction. Creates unshakeable inner core energetic solidity to stabilize you through Earth changes. Acts as a battery, generating, earthing and grounding spiritual energy and power, and enhancing psychic ability and metaphysical gifts. A visionary stone.

The cosmic runway

This particular crystal layout takes you journeying through other dimensions and permanently changes your energetic frequency so that you resonate in sync with the highest potential of these changing times. Alternative crystals are given, so find the ones best attuned to your own unique vibrations. If you are fairly new to crystal working, the opaque forms of high-vibration crystals take you into the higher dimensions more gently. If you do not have the appropriate crystals, you can use the *Crystal Wisdom Oracle* cards, as these carry the energy of the crystals. Build this grid slowly, allowing yourself to attune to and assimilate the energy of each of the crystals as your chakras open.

This layout can also be adapted for journeying through the shamanic worlds. Use Flint, Preseli Bluestone and Stibnite rather than high-vibration Quartzes for a shamanic journey. Again, if you do not have the appropriate crystals you can use the *Crystal Wisdom Oracle* cards or *101 Power Crystals*.

Exercise: Accessing the cosmic runway

You need:

- a grounding crystal such as Elestial Smoky Quartz, Flint or Haematite

- a cosmic anchor crystal such as Boji Stones, Elestial Quartz, Flint, Graphic Smoky Quartz, Haematite, Preseli Bluestone, Selenite, Smoky Brandenberg or Smoky Elestial

- an Alta Major chakra crystal such as Anandalite™, Blue Moonstone

- 6 high-vibration crystals such as Anandalite™, Azeztulite, Brandenberg Amethyst, Nirvana Quartz, Petalite, Phenacite, Rainbow Mayanite, Satyaloka Quartz, Satyamani Quartz, Selenite or Trigonic Quartz

The layout starts with your feet so that you are well grounded and lying down by the time you place the crystals over your head. It can be useful to set a quiet signal to call yourself back after 20 minutes.

✦ Lie in a warm comfortable place so that you can place the crystals on the ground around yourself or ask a friend to do this for you.

✦ Place a Smoky Elestial Quartz or other grounding crystal slightly below and between your feet and consciously invoke your shamanic anchor (see page 12). Tell yourself that your body will remain grounded and centred while you explore other dimensions and that you will return after 20 minutes.

✦ Place two high-vibration crystals at your hips, where you can put your hands on them (use Flint or Stibnite for a shamanic journey).

✦ Place a high-vibration crystal level with or slightly below your shoulders (use Flint or Stibnite for a shamanic journey).

✦ Place a high-vibration crystal at the top of your head. (This is not necessary for a shamanic journey. Instead place Preseli Bluestone on your Soma chakra.)

❖ Consciously invoke your cosmic anchor (*see above*).

❖ Place a high-vibration crystal about a foot above your head. (Not necessary for a shamanic journey.) Feel the Soul Star chakra open.

❖ Place Anandalite™ or Rainbow Mayanite as high as you can reach above your head. (Not necessary for a shamanic journey.) Feel the Stellar Gateway chakra open.

❖ Place an Alta Major chakra opener in the hollow at the base of your skull. (Not necessary for a shamanic journey.)

❖ Close your eyes, relax and place your Brandenberg Amethyst, Preseli Bluestone or other cosmic anchor crystal on the Soma chakra at your hairline. Put your hands on the crystals at your hips and feel yourself lifting out of your physical body into your subtle energy body.

❖ Allow the crystals to take you journeying to your destination.

❖ When it is time to return, slide down your cosmic anchor and settle into your body once more. Take the crystal off your Soma chakra. Feel your subtle energy body settling back into your body, which will realign its energies to accommodate the new frequencies.

❖ Lift your hand up and remove the Anandalite™, put it to one side and picture the Stellar Gateway chakra closing.

❖ Put the Soul Star crystal to one side and feel the Soul Star chakra closing.

❖ Remove the Alta Major chakra crystal from the base of your skull. Sit up slowly. Put the other crystals to one side in the reverse order from which you laid them out. Check that your body has realigned to the new energy and the subtle energy body is incorporated into your physical being. (Anandalite™ on your Soma chakra helps to assimilate and integrate the new energies.)

- ❖ When you reach the Elestial Quartz, put your hands on the crystal and check that your shamanic anchor is in place. If you need to integrate the changes, keep your hands on the crystal and ask it to assist assimilation. Sit quietly allowing the process to complete itself.

- ❖ Thank the crystals for their work.

- ❖ Stand up slowly, stamp your feet and have a warm drink.

SUMMARY ✍

- ❖ Crystals bring about a shift in consciousness, providing access to other dimensions.

- ❖ They can assist in meditation, either singly, as a focus, or via a mandala.

- ❖ High-vibration crystals bring about soul expansion and facilitate journeying to other worlds.

Chapter 17
Crystal divination

The art of using crystals for guidance goes back 5,500 years in written history but many more thousands in practice, as the pouches of stones, polished crystal mirrors and spheres buried with their prehistoric owners attest. Oral tradition tells us that they were used to ascertain and influence the future. To those who are sensitive, holding these artefacts can reveal the distant past.

Early Mesopotamian sources mention an elmeshu stone that functioned as an oracle, which makes the following few lines in an ancient Assyrian private letter rather intriguing: 'To my father say, thus saith *Elmeshu*: Shamash and Marduk fill with wellbeing the days of my father perpetually. My father, be thou well, flourish; the God that preserves my father direct my father's source of grace.'

'Elmeshu' is usually interpreted by archaeologists as a woman, but as Shamash (the Sun) and Marduk (Jupiter) are planetary gods, perhaps they, through the stone, had been consulted as to the future of the writer's father.

Crystal divination continued down the ages. In ancient Greece, Axinomancers placed Agate or Jet onto a red-hot axe to seek out the guilty party in a crime. In the sixth century BCE the Ratnapariksa of Buddhabhatta set out the divinatory meaning of stones. Diamond then, as now, indicated faithful love. In the more recent past, Doctor Dee scryed with a crystal ball to advise Queen Elizabeth I of England.

Methods of divination include drawing crystals or spilling them onto a board, crystal gazing and laying out cards. To obtain the best guidance, use these methods in conjunction with your intuition.

Scrying

Scrying is the art of divining with crystals, or more specifically crystal gazing. In ancient times it was used to reveal the will of the gods. It cannot tell you exactly what your future will be, but if you're at a crossroads, it can show you the outcome of choices and point to which would be most beneficial for you. Always bear in mind that the future is not fixed and unyielding but is being created every moment by your thoughts, beliefs, actions and emotions – and crystals can help you to remain positive and focused on what you wish to manifest.

The accuracy of scrying depends on the skill of the seer, but with a little practice you can soon master this art. It's worth trying several scrying methods to see which suits you.

If the definitive answer to a question is sought, a crystal pendulum, divining gems or crystal oracle cards may be more effective than using a crystal ball or its flatter equivalent, a scrying mirror, as you get a yes or no answer plus timing and guidance. Combining several stones together on a scrying board gives you the bigger picture (*see below*), but my *Crystal Wisdom Oracle* cards give you the deepest insight of all.

Choosing a crystal ball or a scrying mirror

When you gaze into a crystal ball or scrying mirror, your rational mind no longer operates and you focus your intuition. So, when purchasing a crystal ball or scrying mirror, do so when you are in a relaxed and receptive mood.

Exercise: Choosing a crystal ball

✦ Open your palm chakras (*see page 11*).

✦ Handle several balls, but cleanse them first or you'll pick up the vibrations of everyone who has handled them (put some crystal cleanser on your hands).

✦ Feel how heavy they are, how comfortable you are with them.

✦ Look into them and decide whether you prefer a perfectly plain sphere or one that has angles, planes and inclusions within that may help you to see images.

✦ You'll probably find yourself drawn to one in particular – your eyes and hands will keep coming back to it. This is the ball for you.

Practical crystal scrying tips

✦ First clear your mind – a hidden agenda, fears and doubts or an answer you really want will all contaminate scrying, while calm, objective focus produces clear guidance.

✦ Formulate your question carefully. Keep it simple. Get to the essence – ask yourself, 'What lies behind this?' Keep asking until you have reached the core of the question.

✦ Cleanse your crystals before use (*see page 22*).

✦ Harmonize with your crystals. Hold your crystal(s), breathe gently and allow your energies to come into harmony with the stone(s).

✦ Ask your crystals to show you truth. Crystals are living beings that want to cooperate with you, so all you need do is ask. But you might need to remind them that you need clear, unambiguous answers and a timescale!

✦ Try several crystals, especially if you're using a crystal ball, until you know exactly which feels right to you.

✦ Keep your divining crystals in a bag when not in use.

✦ Use the same crystals each time to imbue them with a deeper connection to your intuition.

✦ Keep an open mind! Scrying is notoriously subtle and things are not always what they seem. Don't jump to conclusions too quickly.

✦ Hindsight is the most accurate tool of all, so keep a note of your 'misinterpretations' and consider how they occurred. There is no such thing as a mistake, only a learning experience.

Exercise: Crystal gazing

✦ Have the light source off to one side so that you can see into the crystal. You may like to use candlelight.

✦ When you are in a relaxed state, hold the ball for a few moments to attune it to your vibrations.

✦ Frame your question and consider possible solutions without giving them too much attention.

✦ Place the crystal ball on a black silk or velvet cloth.

✦ Gaze at it with gently focused eyes. It will often appear to mist over. Within the mist, images will form. Don't force them, let them arise naturally.

✦ Watch for pictures appearing either in the crystal or in your mind's eye. The meanings can be positive or negative (*see below*).

✦ When you have finished your session, disconnect your eyes from the ball, briefly cover your third eye with your hand to close it and make a note of what you saw.

✦ Cover your ball with a cloth when not in use.

Do keep a note of what you see, even if it seems to be meaningless. If you persevere, you will understand. Notice the feelings you have, the thoughts that come into your head, the insights that emerge about your life. The crystal can work on a very subtle level to guide you into a more fulfilled future.

Symbolism

The following table includes a list of traditional symbols and their meanings:

Image	Positive	Negative
Eye	Good luck	Bad luck
Moon	New growth	Disappointment
Star	Success	Warning
Globe	Travel	Standstill
Cat	Good luck	Trouble
Dog	Trusty friends	Deceitful friends
Snake	Learning	Betrayal
Bird	A message	Escapism
House	Wellbeing	Financial problems
Tree	Settling down	Loss
Wheel	Travel	Injury

Case history: Seeing true

Clergyman Andrew Lang, president of a psychical research society, wrote a fascinating treatise on crystal balls at the start of the twentieth century. He recorded the following story:

'I had given a glass ball to a young lady, Miss Baillie, who had scarcely any success with it. She lent it to Miss Leslie, who saw a large, square, old-fashioned, red sofa, covered with muslin (which she afterward found in the next country-house she visited). Miss Baillie's brother laughed at these experiments but took the ball into his study, and came back looking "gey gash". He admitted that he had seen a vision – somebody he knew, under a lamp. He said he would discover during the week whether he saw right or not. This was at 5:30 p.m. on a Sunday afternoon.

'On Tuesday Mr Baillie was at a dance in a town
40 miles from his house, and met a Miss Preston.
"On Sunday," he said, "at about half-past five, you
were sitting under a standard lamp, in a dress I never
saw you wear, and a blue blouse with lace over the
shoulders, pouring out tea for a man in blue serge,
whose back was towards me, so that I only saw the tip
of his moustache."

'"Why, the blinds must have been up," said
Miss Preston. "I was at Dulby."'

Crystallomancy

A handful of tumbled crystals can also be used for crystal
divination. Select your tumble stones from those listed
under 'Traditional crystal meanings' below. Semi-precious
stones work just as well as precious gems.

The simplest way is to put the crystals into a bag, shake
them gently, ask your question and either take out the
first two or three that your fingers touch or spill them
onto a board (*see below for meanings*). This gives you
your 'what' answer. 'Timing stones' give you 'when', as
crystals are traditionally associated with days of the week
and months of the year (*see below*). As they are also
linked with countries, they give you 'where' too (*again
see below, adapted from my* Earth Blessings). Before
you look up the meanings, however, take time to softly
focus on the crystals and see if the answer emerges
spontaneously, as this helps you to develop your own
intuitive understanding.

If you are spilling the crystals out onto a board, this table shows the layout of the oracle:

Yes	Future outcome	No
What's standing in the way	Present situation	What will assist
Wrong timing	Past influences	Reframe question

Traditional crystal meanings

- ❖ Agate: worldly success, a journey
    - – Black Agate: courage and prosperity
    - – Red Agate: health and longevity

- ❖ Amber: a voyage

- ❖ Amethyst: life changes and shifts in consciousness

- ❖ Aquamarine: new friends

- ❖ Aventurine: growth and expansion

- ❖ Bloodstone: distressing news is on the way

- ❖ Blue Lace Agate: healing is needed

- ❖ Cat's Eye: beware treachery

- ❖ Chalcedony: friends reunited

- ❖ Chrysoberyl: a time of need

- ❖ Chrysolite: exercise caution

- ❖ Coral: recovery from illness

- ❖ Diamond/Quartz: permanence, love, victory over enemies

- ❖ Emerald/Peridot: much to look forward to
- ❖ Garnet: the solution to a mystery
- ❖ Haematite: new opportunities
- ❖ Jade: immortality and perfection
- ❖ Jasper: earthly affairs are successful, love returned
- ❖ Lapis Lazuli: divine favour
- ❖ Milky/Snow Quartz: profound changes occurring
- ❖ Moonstone: watch out for self-deception or illusions
- ❖ Moss Agate: an unsuccessful journey
- ❖ Onyx: a happy marriage
- ❖ Opal: great possessions
- ❖ Quartz: clarify issues, speak out
- ❖ Rose Quartz: love and self-healing
- ❖ Ruby/Garnet: power and passion, unexpected guests
- ❖ Sapphire: truth and chastity, escape from danger
- ❖ Snowflake Obsidian: the end of a challenging time
- ❖ Tiger's Eye: all is not as it seems
- ❖ Topaz: no harm shall befall you
- ❖ Tourmaline: an accident
- ❖ Turquoise: prosperity, a new job
- ❖ Unakite: compromise and integration are needed

Gems for days of the week

- Sunday: *Ruby*
- Monday: *Moonstone*
- Tuesday: *Coral*
- Wednesday: *Emerald*
- Thursday: *Cat's Eye*
- Friday: *Diamond (Quartz)*
- Saturday: *Sapphire*

Gems for months of the year

- January: *Garnet*
- February: *Amethyst*
- March: *Bloodstone*
- April: *Diamond (Quartz)*
- May: *Emerald*
- June: *Agate*
- July: *Carnelian*
- August: *Sardonyx*
- September: *Sapphire*
- October: *Aquamarine*
- November: *Topaz*
- December: *Turquoise*

State stones and national crystals

A state or national stone supports the energy of that area. As well as being useful indications in divination, such connections can be incorporated into Earth healing layouts (*see page 170*), whether placed on the actual ground or on a map.

Stone	State	Country
Agate	Kentucky, Louisiana, Maryland, Minnesota, Montana, Nebraska, New York, Oregon, South Dakota, Tennessee	Denmark, Panama
Ajoite	Arkansas	-
Amber	-	France, Romania, Sicily
Amethyst	South Carolina	Uruguay
Aragonite	-	Spain
Beryl	New Hampshire	-
Black Fire Opal	Nevada, New South Wales	Hungary
Carnelian	-	Norway, Sweden
Celestite	Pennsylvania	-
Danburite	Connecticut	-
Diamond	-	England, the Netherlands, South Africa
Emerald	North Carolina	Peru, Spain
Flint	Ohio	-
Garnet	Alaska, Connecticut (Almandine Garnet), Idaho (Star Garnet), Vermont (Grossular Garnet)	The Czech Republic, Slovakia

Stone	State	Country
Granite	New Hampshire, North and South Carolina, Vermont, Wisconsin	–
Haematite	Alabama	–
Jade	Alaska, Wyoming	New Zealand, Turkestan
Labradorite	Oregon	–
Lapis Lazuli	–	Bokhara, Bolivia, Chile
Moonstone	Florida	–
Morganite (Pink Beryl)	–	Madagascar
Obsidian	–	Mexico
Peridot	–	Egypt
Quartz	Arkansas, Georgia, Iowa	Switzerland
Rhodochrosite	Colorado	–
Rhodonite	Massachusetts	Russia
Rose Quartz	South Dakota	–
Ruby	–	Myanmar, Thailand
Sapphire	Montana (Montana sapphire)	United States
Serpentine	California, Rhode Island	
Smoky Quartz	New Hampshire	Scotland
Sunstone	Oregon	–
Topaz	Texas (blue), Utah (yellow)	–
Tourmaline	Maine	Brazil
Turquoise	Arizona, Nevada, New Mexico	Iran, Turkey
Zincite	–	Poland

The Crystal Wisdom Oracle

My *Crystal Wisdom Oracle* card and book pack offers you a way to divine with crystals without needing the stones themselves. The cards help you to know yourself and can guide you on your life path. Exploring past, present and future influences, the pack draws on crystals used for divination and healing for thousands of years and introduces new high-vibration stones to expand your consciousness and access different dimensions. The cards can also be used to bring wellbeing to your body.

Illustrated with superb photographs that radiate the very essence of the crystals, this deck is designed to help you speak to your soul for guidance and the answers are at two levels: self-understanding and divination.

The Crystal Wisdom cards are divided into four Vibrations: Earthy, Healing, Cosmic and Integration. Earthy crystals work well at the material level of being, the physical body and the world around you, while exceptionally high-vibration Cosmic ones operate at the level of the soul and open your intuition. Healing Vibrations assist you in understanding the effect of your mind and your soul's needs on your body and show you how to return to a state of wellbeing. There are also crystals that bridge the material and subtle worlds. These are Integration crystals and their job is to step down higher frequencies and step up your vibrations so that you integrate the guidance.

Case history: What will help me recover?

After several years in a successful but highly stressful career and a traumatic relationship break-up, Kylie plunged into deep depression. She set out the Oracle in a Square lattice:

Intention/situation

Card: Malachite – the subconscious mind

Self-understanding: Unconscious programs or beliefs are running your life and may cause psychosomatic dis-ease. Go willingly into the depths – therapy may be needed. Your deepest fears become your greatest gifts as hidden abilities come to light.

Divination: Stand firm in your power. You will survive. Spread your wings.

What's holding you back

Card: Ajoite – Compassionate being

Self-understanding: Find your core of ultimate peace and universal love. Let the crystal transmute toxic emotions and old grief, replacing them with forgiveness, compassion and serenity.

Divination: Put down your burdens, knowing you are a being of light. Resolve conflicts and forgive those who have wounded you. Let go of the pain of the past or betrayal. Let your compassion encompass everyone. Charity or volunteer work is indicated.

Action required

Card: Lavender Aragonite – Environmental healing

Self-understanding: Lavender Aragonite says, 'Become comfortable in your own body and in your environment.' You incarnated with a specific purpose in mind, which was to be a guardian for the Earth. But you also need to pay attention to where you live within yourself.

Outcome

Card: Garnet – Constancy

Self-understanding: Recognize that you have a passionate soul with a strong, courageous heart. It is time to be confident and constant. Let go of your inner demons, taboos, inhibitions and fantasies, recognize where you sabotage yourself and expand your awareness into all that you can be. Virtue matters to you and you are capable of great devotion to a cause and have a strong survival instinct.

Divination: The time for action is now. Turn a crisis into a learning challenge. Be emotionally honest with yourself and others. You attract a partner for sexual healing.

Kylie decided to attend college to retrain and also undertook a course of cognitive behavioural therapy that brought a different perspective into her life. She realized that the environment that she had to heal was her own inner one. She found a relationship with a man who was fun and didn't 'do my head in'. She volunteered at a dog rescue centre and found a home that nourished her. Now her college course has been a success and she intends to go on to university. She is well on the way to healing her depression and changing her life.

SUMMARY ✍️

* Methods of crystal divination include drawing crystals or spilling them onto a board, crystal gazing or laying out cards.

* To obtain the best guidance, use these methods in conjunction with your intuition.

Chapter 18
The Crystal Zodiac

There has been a link between crystals and the zodiac for thousands of years. The thirteenth-century *Lapidary of Alfonso X*, King of Castile, set out the relationship between the signs of the zodiac and crystals in addition to their medicinal and magical properties. Each degree of each sign related to a stone, and the astrological planets in turn related to particular stones. The strength of the crystals' properties was said to vary with the movements of the heavenly bodies overhead. But this in turn was based on a much older system.

Crystals and the zodiac signs

The zodiac is divided into 12 sections, each with its own characteristics and its own crystal or crystals. Your own 'birthstone', the stone of your birth sign, helps you to make the most of that sign and overcome any challenges you have. However, there is no consensus on exactly which birthstones fit which signs. Traditionally, crystals and gemstones were linked to specific planets and zodiac signs because the energies resonated and there were colour correspondences, but the discovery of new crystals has opened the way for a deeper connection between Earth and sky and each sign now has a myriad of crystals associated with it.

We'll look more closely at the individual signs later, but first let's explore the roots of the birthstone tradition.

Birthstones Ancient and Modern

A commonly used table of birthstones, adopted in 1912, is that of the American Jewellers' Association. It indicates the worldwide foundations of the tradition. The following table gives some indication of how widespread this is and also includes modern birthstones.

Birth Month	Modern Birthstones	Ancient and Traditional Birthstones			
		Hebrew birthstones	Roman birthstones	Arabic birthstones	Hindu birthstones
January	Garnet	Garnet	Garnet	Garnet	Ruby
February	Amethyst	Amethyst	Amethyst	Amethyst	Topaz
March	Aqua-marine, Bloodstone	Bloodstone	Bloodstone	Bloodstone	Opal
April	Diamond	Sapphire	Sapphire	Sapphire	Diamond
May	Emerald	Agate	Agate	Emerald	Emerald
June	Moonstone, Pearl	Emerald	Emerald	Agate	Pearl
July	Ruby	Onyx	Onyx	Carnelian	Sapphire
August	Peridot	Carnelian	Carnelian	Sardonyx	Ruby
September	Sapphire	Peridot	Peridot	Peridot	Zircon
October	Opal, Tourmaline	Aqua-marine	Aqua-marine	Aqua-marine	Coral
November	Citrine, Yellow Topaz	Yellow Topaz	Yellow Topaz	Yellow Topaz	Cat's eye
December	Blue Topaz, Turquoise	Ruby	Ruby	Ruby	Topaz

The Breastplate of the High Priest

In most crystal books – and on the American Jewellers' Association website – you'll be told that birthstones stem from the Breastplate of the High Priest. This was the ritual vestment with 12 gemstones that the high priest Aaron wore after Moses received the Ten Commandments. After extensive academic research, however, I can say this is unlikely to have established the exact stones. Translators can't even agree on which crystals were in the breastplate.

The instructions for fabricating the breastplate are in Exodus 28, 15–30:

> *And thou shall make the breastplate of judgement with cunning work...*
> *And thou shalt set in it settings of stones, even four rows of stones:*
> *The first row shall be a sardius [sardonyx], a topaz, and a carbuncle [garnet]*
> *And the second row shall be an emerald, a sapphire, and a diamond.*
> *And the third row a ligure, an agate, and an amethyst.*
> *And the fourth row a beryl, and an onyx, and a jasper.*
> KING JAMES VERSION

'Emerald' was probably Green Aventurine or Green Feldspar, as Emeralds were only mined in the area much later. 'Sapphire', unknown in that part of the ancient world, was probably Lapis Lazuli brought from Afghanistan across ancient trade routes. The New Revised Standard Version of the Bible translates the stones as:

> *A row of carnelian, chrysolite and emerald*
> *A turquoise, a sapphire and a moonstone*
> *A jacinth [ziron], agate and amethyst,*
> *A beryl, onyx and jasper.*

Each stone corresponded to one of the 12 tribes of Israel. Those stones later became linked to the signs of the zodiac and/or the months of the year, drawing on an ancient Mesopotamian precedent. The prophet Ezekiel tells the neighbouring King of Tyre, sometimes mistakenly believed to be Satan (*see 'Are Crystals Ungodly?' on my website*):

> *You were in Eden, the garden of God*
> *Adorned with gems of every kind: sarin and chrysolite*
> *and jade, topaz, cornelian and green jasper, lapis lazuli,*
> *purple garnet and green feldspar... and the spandles*
> *you wore were made for you on the day of your birth;*
> *you were God's holy hill and you walked proudly*
> *among stones that flashed with fire.*
> Ezekiel 28, 13–15

By the time Flavius Josephus, a Roman historian, was writing in the first century CE, the connection between birthstones and the breastplate was regarded as accepted fact and it has been carried forward into the present day. (*See my website for a deeper investigation and for Josephus' description of the breastplate in use as an oracle.*)

How do birthstones work?

Traditionally, crystals were linked to specific zodiac signs because the energy of the stone resonated with that sign, or because the planet connected with the sign or month was represented by the crystal. Lusty Mars, for instance, whose colour is red, rules fiery Aries and April. Mars and red are linked to the passionate Ruby and red Haematite. Mars is also one of Scorpio's co-rulers, and Ruby is a companion crystal for that sexy sign.

In the Middle Ages astrology was closely linked to medicine, remedies being prescribed according to planetary indications. Paracelsus (1493–1591) suggested that this is 'the science which teaches one to know the stars, what the heaven of each may be, how the heaven has produced man at his conception, and in the same way constellated him'. In modern times the link was explained by the astrologer Kaplan:

> *'Crystals and most gemstones are formed by a crystalline structure that functions as a building block, or building system, in creation. All aspects of creation correspond to each other... trace elements found within crystals and gemstones are also found within our bodies. When you wear a stone, the trace elements in the stone work in correspondence to and stimulate the trace elements in your body.'*

This is a statement with which ancient crystal workers would have concurred, although they believed that the planetary gods had a hand in it as well.

The signs and their stones

Each sign is on its own unique journey of self-discovery, a journey that can be expedited by the judicious application of crystals. They help bring out the innate potential of a sign, overcome its challenges and harmonize discordances.

Aries

Dates: 21 March to 19 April
Birthstones: Diamond, Ruby
Ruby helps you to project your true self out into the world, bringing out your courage. It emanates passion and vitality, spicing up life. The stone aligns ideals and the will, enabling you to focus on the task ahead. You don't suffer fools gladly and Ruby draws anger to the surface for dissipation. It may even overheat situations, bringing you into the danger on which you thrive. It may also make you more self-centred and self-absorbed. The calming influence of Diamond offsets this by stimulating thoughtfulness and consideration for others. Diamond also helps to overcome a tendency to put yourself first in all things.

Paradoxically, procrastination can be a problem for you. Many projects are started, but few completed. Any hesitancy is quickly overcome by fiery Ruby, which assists in harnessing leadership qualities to perseverance and gently diffuses explosive situations. This stone maximizes your potential for decisive action. It helps in righting wrongs and fighting for a good cause.

Taurus

20 April to 20 May
Birthstones: Emerald, Peridot
Emerald encourages enjoying life to the full. It is voluptuous Venus's favourite stone. Outwardly, you are a sensible and pragmatic soul, inwardly you are sensual and hedonistic, relishing all the good things of life, ruled by Venus and valuing comfort above all. You hate change and this birthstone promotes enduring partnership. Emerald is

'the stone of successful love' and wearing it helps you find loyalty and domestic bliss. Said to protect against enchantment, it changes colour during unfaithfulness.

Emerald's infinite patience resonates with your nature, but there are times when this patient approach to life becomes a handicap. Peridot is the stone *par excellence* for facilitating necessary change and ameliorating your legendary jealousy. You have powerful emotions which can be deeply entrenched, especially resentment and possessiveness. These dissolve under Peridot, which assists forgiveness and fosters reconciliation. You seek inner security rather than external safety, and Emerald illuminates the spiritual pathway.

Gemini

21 May to 20 June
Birthstones: Agate, Tourmaline
You are extremely active, physically and mentally, and your innate ability to multi-task is strengthened by Agate. This stable and grounding stone encourages paying precise attention to details while still seeing the bigger picture. It brings hidden information to light. It is also invaluable in avoiding the nervous tension to which you are prone. However, it works slowly, which can trigger impatience. Tourmaline works faster and balances the two sides of the brain, integrating the inner and outer selves. It stabilizes a tendency to fly off in too many directions at once.

Communication is your forte – gathering an enormous amount of information from disparate sources. With Agate's assistance, the essence is distilled and you can make inspired intuitive connections. Agate also overcomes any tendency to speak without thought of the consequences. One of your major challenges is in identifying what exactly is truth, and Agate promotes integrity and truthfulness.

Cancer

21 June to 22 July
Birthstones: Moonstone, Pearl
A 'stone of new beginnings', Moonstone is connected to intuition. You are highly sensitive and prone to mood swings, and Moonstone keeps you emotionally balanced. It attunes to your own unique biorhythm cycle. Pearl is a convenient stone to wear at full moon, when Moonstone may be too strong.

You are highly ambitious, although it is well hidden, and the passion and energy of Pearl propel you forward and attract an outlet for hidden talents.

As a sign that values routine and hesitates to make changes, you may find that life becomes static. Moonstone opens the possibility of serendipity and synchronicity – and heightens concentration.

As a water sign, you pick up other people's thoughts and feelings very easily, and confuse them with your own. Moonstone may exacerbate this tendency, but Black Moonstone will help you to differentiate. It also teaches that what you put out comes back and assists your soul pathway, which is to nurture without enabling.

Leo

23 July to 22 August
Birthstones: Cat's or Tiger's Eye
The ostentation of the rare and beautiful Cat's Eye radiates benevolent warmth. Tiger's Eye is an excellent, cheaper alternative. This stone helps you to shine. It combines the energy of the Earth with that of the sun to create a grounded and yet high vibration. The golden form in particular resonates with your sunny self. Tiger's Eye is protective and facilitates constructive manifestation of your strong will. It also ameliorates your considerable pride.

You are a highly creative sign known for your vigour and vitality, although, as a fixed sign, you need a stimulus to move in a new direction. Tiger's Eye pushes beyond limitations and its vibrant energy stimulates your natural generosity. This stone of abundance helps you to recognize inner riches as well as drawing support and facilitates using power wisely. This is not power over others, but rather self-empowerment.

Virgo

23 August to 22 September
Birthstones: Peridot, Sardonyx
Virgo values integrity and virtuous conduct, and Sardonyx resonates to these qualities. Strong and stable, it supports the search for meaningful existence. The livelier Peridot supports razor-sharp perception, assisting in letting go of habits that block growth. It encourages kindness to yourself – an essential ingredient in overcoming your Virgoan tendency towards self-criticism. You seek perfection and

set incredibly high goals. With Peridot's help, mistakes are accepted as a learning experience.

You have an enormous capacity to be of service, which sometimes means personal needs and aspirations are put on hold. Peridot takes you out of the 'servitude trap', teaching that true service comes from the heart, doing what is necessary without thought of reward but not being put upon by others.

Libra

23 September to 22 October
Birthstones: Opal, Sapphire
The vibrant hue of Sapphire brings dreams to fruition and imbues life with lightness and joy, restoring equilibrium. This 'stone of peace' resonates with your desire for tranquillity. Furthermore, you are partial to a sybaritic lifestyle, valuing quality, aesthetics and good taste, and Sapphire's ability to attract prosperity is useful to you.

Diplomatic, with a flair for creating harmony, it is in negotiation and resolution that you shine, and Opal, another of your birthstones, harmonizes conflict and assists in expressing opinions.

An Opal ring signifies faithfulness in love. Opal amplifies traits, good or bad, bringing them up so that you achieve the perfection you seek. You are a laid-back sign that prefers ease to inner work. Opal smoothes your way, particularly as this stone stimulates creativity and releases inhibitions. This iridescent crystal also opens up the intuitive side of your nature.

Your image is particularly important to you, as you want to look good and have others think well of you. If your self-image is a little low, Opal enhances it and encourages a positive outlook.

One of your greatest challenges is to avoid becoming a people pleaser. You opt for a quiet life, backing away from confrontation, and you need approval, so may put other people's needs first. But, as astute observers observe, you are also quietly ruthless, although you hide your innate selfishness better than other people. Eventually, something will have to give. Opal and Sapphire both ensure congruency between personal needs and those of others, releasing the authentic self from 'sugary-sweet niceness'.

Scorpio

23 October to 21 November
Birthstones: Malachite, Turquoise

Malachite brings about transformation at all levels and is especially effective psychologically. You handle this stone's forcefulness with ease. Empathetic Turquoise balances the powerfulness of Malachite, bringing inner calm. This purification stone enhances intuition and provides protection whilst you explore the spiritual and darker realms. But, beware, Turquoise has the ability to change colour in the presence of infidelity and, despite loyalty to a partner, you are not the most faithful of signs.

Controlling the sting in your tail can also be a challenge, which Malachite may exacerbate, as it gets straight to the point, but Turquoise holds back verbal assaults and curtails intolerance, helping you to be less acerbic.

You go where others fear to tread, and Malachite is an excellent stone for accessing inner riches. Your ability to diagnose and see below the surface also makes you a natural healer, which Malachite and Turquoise support.

Sagittarius

22 November to 21 December
Birthstones: Topaz, Turquoise
Topaz is an excellent companion on your eternal quest for knowledge. It promotes trust in the universe and teaches how to *be* rather than do. This stone's vibrant energy brings joy, generosity and all good things, facilitating the attainment of goals, while Turquoise offers protection and attunes you to the spiritual realms.

You have an unfortunate tendency to blurt things out, but Turquoise facilitates unblocking the throat chakra and thinking before speaking, while your incredibly active questing mind benefits from Topaz, as it encourages seeing the bigger picture and the minute details and recognizing how they interrelate.

Capricorn

22 December to 19 January
Birthstones: Garnet, Onyx
Yours is a serious, rule-orientated sign, enlivened by a strong sense of humour. Onyx provides the authority you crave and offers support in difficult times. However, it can make you somewhat too self-controlled and 'heavy'. Fortunately, Garnet infuses lightness. It is a revitalizing stone which brings serenity or passion as appropriate. It inspires the

love and devotion you seek, promoting commitment and fidelity.

You have a great desire for wealth and status, and whilst Garnet attracts these, it never allows them to take over. This stone fills you with enthusiasm and confidence and brightens your pathway, while Onyx offers the gift of wise decisions.

You also have a strong sex drive, and Garnet invigorates libido, removes inhibitions and aids sexual potency.

Aquarius

20 January to 18 February
Birthstones: Aquamarine, Moonstone
Many of you live in the future, from where you bring back insights to assist the evolution of humankind. Aquamarine promotes spiritual awareness and service to humanity, aligning purpose to experience. Its calming energy is excellent for reducing the stress to which you are prone. Your potential, and your challenge, is to bring about social change and justice for everyone. Moonstone assists.

Aquarian emotions can be unstable and irrational. Moonstone soothes emotional instability and stress, but it may be too strong at full moon, so use Aquamarine then. A powerful emotional healer, this stone dissolves old emotional patterning. If you feel alienated from others, it is beneficial. It is excellent for calming and focusing the mind. Removing extraneous thoughts, it filters the information reaching the brain.

Pisces

19 February to 20 March
Birthstones: Amethyst, Blue Lace Agate

You move fluidly between everyday reality, fantasy, imagination and spiritual mysticism. Amethyst forms the bridge. With a tendency to absorb emanations from other people, you need its protection. Boundaries are a difficult issue for you and this crystal is invaluable for establishing them and helping you to feel safe.

Most of you indulge in half-truths and escapism. Amethyst helps you to overcome this tendency. Your most difficult challenge is avoiding victim-martyr-saviour-rescuer-persecutor situations and this stone assists in avoiding that trap.

You have considerable psychic and artistic gifts, and Amethyst hones intuition. Blue Lace Agate is the seer's stone, heightening awareness of hidden worlds and keeping you on a positive track. If you are a Pisces man, Blue Lace Agate assists in accepting your sensitive, feeling nature.

SUMMARY

- There has been a link between crystals and the zodiac for thousands of years. The discovery of new crystals has now opened the way for a deeper connection between Earth and sky.

- Birthstones help you to make the most of your zodiac sign and overcome any challenges you have. Each sign now has a myriad of crystals associated with it.

Chapter 19
Higher connections

Crystals can help us make connections with higher beings, both angels and crystal mentors, or oversouls, who hold the energy of each type of crystal.

Angels

Crystals have traditional connections with angels. Angels vibrate at a higher frequency than that of the Earth, which is why crystals are a useful intermediary.

Guardian angels aren't merely vaguely religious figures somewhere 'out there' – they're dynamic figures who assist you with your life. Invoking your guardian angel is particularly useful if you are walking in a dark place, if you have a difficult task to perform or if you're meeting someone with whom there is a conflict. But it's no use waiting until you need your angel before you try to make contact – do it now!

There are several crystals that assist you in making contact with angelic beings. Choose one from the list below or use a stone you've picked up that speaks of angels to you.

Crystals for angelic contact

Ajoite, Amphibole, Anandalite™, Angel's Hair (Rutilated Quartz), Angelite, Aquamarine, Candle Quartz, Celestite, Danburite, Dumortierite, Lemurian Seed, Morganite, Muscovite, Pariaba Tourmaline, Phantom Quartz, Selenite, Tanzanite, Tanzine or other Aura Quartzes, Tugtupite, White Elestial Quartz, White Flint

Celestite

Vibration: High

Celestite links to the angelic realms and your guardian angel and stimulates spiritual insights. Its ethereal blue brings about profound inner peace, dispersing anxieties, calming incandescent emotions and promoting clarity of mind.

Exercise: Meeting your guardian angel

✦ Spend a few moments relaxing, breathing gently and evenly and letting any tension flow out of your body through your hands and feet. Hold your angelic crystal in your hand and place it over your heart.

✦ When you're ready, picture a shaft of light coming down in front of you and reaching into your heart. This shaft of light reaches from the high-vibration angelic realms down to the Earth plane. Ask your guardian angel to travel down this shaft of light to meet you.

✦ When your angel arrives, feel it move round to stand behind you, wrapping you in protective wings.

✦ Spend as long as you like with your angel, building up trust and enjoying the sense of protection. Ask your angel to be with you whenever you need protection or guidance. Affirm to yourself that this is so.

✦ Ask the angel to make a powerful connection to your crystal so that whenever you hold the crystal, your angel is present.

✦ Thank your angel for being there.

✦ The shaft of light recedes back to the angelic realms. Before opening your eyes, check you are enclosed in a bubble of light and that the Earth Star chakra beneath your feet is open and grounding you.

✦ When you are ready, bring your attention fully back into the room and open your eyes.

Note: You can adapt this exercise to meet other angelic beings, such as the angel of healing, or to receive guidance.

The crystal mentors

All crystals have higher beings, crystal mentors or oversouls (as Michael Eastwood of Aristia has named them), who hold the energy of that type of crystal. They have an interconnected hive mind that accesses the whole. They are the consciousness that fills the spaces between the atoms of the crystal. They are anxious to make contact and will happily guide you in your crystal work and your daily life.

Exercise: Meeting a crystal mentor

✦ Sit comfortably and hold your crystal in your hands or put it where you can comfortably gaze into it (use a *Crystal Wisdom Oracle* or *Crystal Oversoul* card if you do not have a crystal).

❖ Invite the crystal mentor to make itself known to you.

❖ Half close your eyes and gaze at the crystal or the card.

❖ Open your third eye chakra and feel the crystal energy taking it to a higher frequency. Feel yourself wrapped in crystal love.

❖ Be open to the crystal mentor communicating with you through images, intuitions, thoughts, impressions, feelings or bodily sensations.

❖ When you have finished, thank the crystal mentor for its guidance and break off contact, but be aware that you can reconnect at any time.

SUMMARY ✍

❖ Crystals can be used to make contact with higher beings.

❖ They have traditional connections with angels.

❖ Angels vibrate at a higher frequency than the Earth, which is why crystals are a useful intermediary.

❖ The more conscious you are of your guardian angel and the more you call on this beautiful being, the more protection you'll receive.

❖ All crystals have oversouls, or mentors, who hold the energy of that specific type of crystal.

❖ These crystal mentors are also waiting to share their wisdom and assist you in every way possible.

Chapter 20
Crystal skulls

Crystal skulls have taken on an aura of magic and mystery like no other crystal artefacts. They can be amazing tools for personal and planetary evolution if used with the right intention and metaphysical care.

Skulls in the modern world

Some of the crystal skulls around today are claimed to be ancient artefacts assisting the evolution of humankind. They are said to be between 5,000 and 30,000 years old, remnants of the lost continents of Atlantis and Lemuria. Others are modern copies that can be activated for communication and guidance.

The ancient skulls are believed to be making themselves known again to share their wisdom. However, their keepers emphasize that this will only happen once humankind has evolved sufficiently to understand the spiritual implications. In the meantime, keepers with appropriate training and sensitivity communicate with the skulls and pass on their messages. But you can work with modern skulls and receive insights for yourself.

Traditionally, skulls are of Clear Quartz, but they need not be. They are now being carved in just about every known crystal and every size and shape. Not only human skulls are available – skulls of dragons and other animals abound.

Each mineral brings a particular quality to the skull. My Lapis Lazuli dragon skull is attuned to the highest wisdom, while my Smoky Quartz skull works with Earth healing. My Sedona Stone head positively zings with energy, and my Agate skull takes great delight in pricking bubbles of pretentiousness. Its message is 'Get real.' Try out several skulls before settling on yours.

Also, as with all things esoteric and crystal, remember that discrimination and common sense are needed when interacting with the skulls. It cannot be assumed that the beings inhabiting them are necessarily working for the highest good, nor should it be taken for granted that all is as it seems. Not all the guidance is of the highest quality. There may be trickery and deception as well. You may be told what you want to hear and, like all crystals, skulls can only work at the level of your vibrations. So, check out your skull carefully before believing all that is imparted.

Case history: Meeting the skulls

There is no denying, however, the seductive qualities of crystal skulls and the impact they have on your spiritual evolution. I met my first one in 1976 in the Museum of Mankind in London. I stood entranced in front of it for two hours while viewing the far past. It felt as though only a few minutes had gone by. However, it was many years before I purchased my first skull. Now

I have a growing conclave. They enable me to change my vibrational frequency and journey through many dimensions then ground the wisdom gained.

The legend of the 13 skulls

A Mesoamerican myth from the Mayan and Aztec civilizations tells of 13 crystal skulls belonging to the Goddess of Death. Known as 'the mothers and fathers of wisdom', each was carved from a single piece of crystal and had a moveable jaw. They reflected the view that death was just a doorway to another dimension. On death, the spirit would rejoin the ancestors and the body would return to fertilize Mother Earth. These ancient skulls not only carried hidden wisdom but also had the gift of telepathy and healing. Guarded by keeper-priests, each was kept at a different sacred site.

In other versions of the legend, 13 major skulls have authority over a total of 52 spread throughout the world. Cherokee Indians are said to have a similar legend in which 12 of the skulls belong to each of 12 inhabited planets within the cosmos, with the thirteenth acting as a bridge between the different worlds.

The Mitchell-Hedges skull: Ancient artefact or modern copy?

The best-known, and most controversial, crystal skull is that allegedly found by the late Anna Mitchell-Hedges at her father's archaeological dig in Central America. She claimed that on her seventeenth birthday in April 1927 she discovered a crystal skull lacking its lower jaw under a ruined altar. The jaw was later found close by and was a perfect fit, having been carved from a single piece of Quartz.

It has been shown that Anna Mitchell-Hedges was not even at the dig on her birthday, but whether this is disinformation is not known – many people claim that it is. She maintained up to her death that she had discovered the skull at Lubaantun, the Place of the Fallen Stones, but there is evidence to suggest that her father purchased a late nineteenth-century skull at an auction at Sotheby's in London in 1943, and it may be that this is the origin of the Mitchell-Hedges skull. Opinions vary and it is hotly contested as to whether the skull is a fake or an authentic ancient artefact.

What is not in doubt, however, is that the skull has taken on a life of its own. It is reputed to speak, to have a distinctive aura around it and to contain images of past, present and future. Other skulls round the world have certainly done this, creating an energy network rather like a crystal internet. These skulls are communicating to people all around the globe the need to honour Mother Earth.

Accessing your crystal skull

If you own a crystal or stone skull and it has not yet started to communicate with you, a simple attunement will harmonize your vibrational frequency with that of the skull and activate its energy.

Exercise: Connecting with your crystal skull

❖ First cleanse your crystal skull. If there is a genuine higher being already within it, cleansing it will not dissolve the contact. If there is a lesser being, the information you receive is unlikely to be of value. Use a proprietary crystal cleanser or immerse the skull in salt or running water (unless it is friable or delicate, in which case place it in brown rice overnight).

❖ If the skull needs recharging, place it in sunlight or use a proprietary recharger.

❖ Open your palm chakras and place your hands on either side of the skull. Wait a few moments. If the skull feels 'empty', invite the highest possible being to enter it and communicate with you. If it feels 'full', invite the being within to make itself known to you. Always ask that what you are shown is truth and for the highest good of all.

❖ Place the skull in front of you, preferably level with your eyes. With softly focused eyes, gaze into its eye sockets. Ask that it communicate with you in a language you understand. Notice any sensations around your head. Prickling or buzzing is quite common.

❖ If your skull is clear crystal, gaze into it to see pictures or receive communications. If it is opaque, place your hands on it and allow images to form in your mind's eye or words to be heard in your inner ear. Acknowledge any thoughts or pictures that spontaneously rise up into your awareness.

❖ When you have completed the session, disconnect your awareness and cover your third eye briefly to close it down. Put your skull away, then record your impressions.

SUMMARY

+ Crystal skulls can be obtained in a variety of materials.

+ Some are claimed to be ancient artefacts assisting the evolution of humankind. Others are modern copies that can be activated for communication and guidance.

Chapter 21
Living the crystal way

We've reached the last chapter and it's time to bring all your crystal knowledge together and integrate it.

Many years ago I wrote:

'And finally, if you want to change your life, find yourself one of the new Shift Crystals. These amazing high-energy crystals formed from Quartz that was laid down on Calcite. The Calcite then dissolved away, leaving fissures and caverns studded with beautiful crystals. When one was first put into my hand, I simply could not let go of it. For years I had used a visualization of travelling into a crystal cave when leading meditations to find your soul purpose. Now that crystal cave was in my hand and I could feel all my old programming dropping away and the energies quite literally shifting as I attuned to my purpose. It was a moment for which I had been preparing all my life.'

This experience brought about profound – and rapid – changes. Some were welcome, others not so at the time, but all were purposeful and part of my spiritual evolution. Sadly, as with so many crystals that come into play for a short time, do their work and then retire, there are few Shift Crystals around these days (though I still have my 'crystal cave' and you can tune in to its vibrations from afar via the picture on my Facebook page, Crystal Judy Hall). But fortunately many of the new high-vibration finds have taken over that role and have lifted my energies – and my understanding – way beyond what I thought possible back then. I look on it as an ever-expanding ladder of crystal energies that reaches into other dimensions and opens infinite possibilities.

So, how do you integrate crystal energy into your own life? It's simple:

- Play with your crystals!

- Spend joyful time with them, meditate and listen to what they have to say.

- Wear your crystals. Let them impart their energies and raise your vibrations on a daily basis.

- Surround yourself with just enough crystals. Don't overdo it! (Anyone who has been in my home will laugh at this, but you need to find the right number of harmonious crystals for you.)

- Use crystal grids to create safe and sacred space, protection and energy enhancement.

- Whenever you feel slightly off-balance, ask your crystals which one wants to work with you to bring back equilibrium and offer you healing.

✦ Use your crystals for environmental healing at every opportunity.

✦ Attune to the crystal mentors and let them guide your life and your spiritual evolution.

✦ Be open to new crystals finding you. The majority of my most exciting crystals have arrived serendipitously. Turn on your heartlight and draw them to you.

✦ And finally, don't forget to send crystal energy and healing to our planet, thanking it for bringing these crystal treasures to your notice and helping it to regain its equilibrium.

SUMMARY

✦ Crystals aren't something separate and apart – make them part of your daily life.

✦ Once you attune to crystal energy, the changes in your awareness are rapid and your life opens out in unexpected ways.

✦ Living the crystal way means interacting with your crystals on a daily basis. Have them around you, talk to them, make them a part of your life – and share the energy with those around you to uplift the whole.

Conclusion
'With sweet converse smooth the rugged road'

The ancient *Lithica*, from which many of the chapter headings in this book are taken, is the story of a crystal initiation. So too is this book itself. By now you have been initiated into the mysteries of crystals and your awareness has opened. You have learned to communicate with the crystal beings.

The *Lithica* concludes with the words:

And we, whilst yet bourn far distant showed,
Thus with sweet converse smoothed the rugged road.

New crystals will no doubt go on being discovered, many with even higher vibrations than those we know now. It has been my experience that the more open to this experience you are, the more you attract these new crystals to you. When this happens to you, play with them. Enjoy their incredible vibes and the support they offer you. Let them enhance your life and bring peace to your environment.

And share your knowledge with others who are on the same path. Doing so can only uplift the whole planet.

Enjoy your crystals.

Glossary

Aura: the subtle energy body around the physical body, comprising physical, emotional, mental, ancestral, karmic and spiritual layers.

Biomagnetic energy: a subtle, organized electromagnetic energy field around living things.

Bioscalar energy/waves: an energy field created when two electromagnetic fields counteract each other, which directly influences tissue at the microscopic level, bringing about healing balance.

Cellular memory: memory, carried by the cells, of past-life or ancestral attitudes, trauma and patterns that have become deeply ingrained.

Chakra: an energy linkage point between the physical and subtle bodies.

Core beliefs: ancient, deeply held, often unconscious beliefs that have been passed down through the ancestral line or the soul's lineage.

Crystal mentors or oversouls: the hive-mind beings that inhabit crystals and work from other dimensions, communicating across space, time and distance.

Dantien: a small, spirally rotating, power-generating sphere sitting on top of the sacral chakra.

Dis-ease: the state which results from physical imbalances, blocked feelings, suppressed emotions and negative thinking and which, if not reversed, leads to illness.

Earth healing: rectifying the distortion of the Earth's energy field or meridian grid caused by pollution, electromagnetic interference and the destruction of its resources.

Electromagnetic smog: a subtle but detectable electromagnetic field given off by power lines and electrical equipment that has an adverse effect on sensitive people.

EMF: electromagnetic frequency.

Essence: the energetic vibrations of a crystal that have been transferred to water by immersing the crystal in spring water and placing it in sunlight, then bottled with a preservative.

Expanded awareness/consciousness: an expanded spectrum of consciousness that encompasses the grounded, lower frequencies of Earth and the higher frequencies of other dimensions. It facilitates accessing each and every level of reality and all time-frames simultaneously.

Geopathic stress and geopathogens: Earth and physiological stress created by energy disturbance from underground water, power lines, ley lines and other subterranean events.

Grids/gridding: placing crystals around a building, person or place for energy enhancement or protection (the position is best dowsed for).

Grounding: creating a strong connection between your soul, your physical body and the Earth.

Healing challenge: when the symptoms of dis-ease are exacerbated before they get better.

High vibration: high-vibration crystals resonate at a lighter, finer, higher frequency that reaches higher-dimensional consciousness.

Inclusion: a speck or plate of another mineral within a crystal.

Inner levels: levels of being that encompass intuition, psychic awareness, archetypes, emotions, feelings, the subconscious mind and subtle energies.

Interface: where two energy fields meet.

Journeying: when the soul leaves the physical body and travels to distant locations.

Lapidary: a book outlining the properties of crystals.

Lightbody: a subtle energy body vibrating at a very high frequency.

Matrix: the rock in which a crystal forms.

Mental influences: the effects of other people's thoughts and strong opinions on your mind.

Meridian: a subtle energy channel that runs close to the surface of the skin, or the planet, and contains acupuncture points.

Negative emotional programming: 'oughts' and 'shoulds' and emotions such as guilt, instilled often in childhood or other lives, that remain in the subconscious mind and influence present behaviour.

Psychic attack/ill-wishing: malevolent thoughts or feelings towards another person, whether consciously or unconsciously directed.

Psychic vampirism: feeding on the energy of others.

Qi: the life force that energizes the physical and subtle bodies.

Shamanic anchor: an energy conduit hooked into the centre of the Earth.

Soul: vehicle for carrying the eternal spirit.

Soul plan/life plan: the soul's intention and plan of learning for the present life.

Subtle bodies: layers of the aura.

Thought forms: energetic forms created by strong positive or negative thoughts that affect mental functioning.

Resources

The crystals from this book are displayed in colour on www.judyhall.co.uk and www.angeladditions.co.uk

Jasper tie-cutters and rare high-vibration crystals are available from www.angeladditions.co.uk (e-mail for details).

Crystal suppliers

www.angeladditions.co.uk (Judy Hall crystals)

www.exquisitecrystals.com (USA)

www.ksccrystals.com (UK)

www.neatstuff.net/avalon/q-to-s/Rainbow-Mayanite-Quartz.html (Rainbow Mayanite, USA)

www.hehishelo.co.uk (UK)

Music

The Crystal Experience has a CD with specially written music to enhance your crystal attunement, or use any meditative CD.

Further reading

Books by Judy Hall

Crystal Prescriptions: The A–Z guide to over 1,200 symptoms and their healing crystals (O Books, 2005)

The Encyclopedia of Crystals and Healing Stones: The definitive guide to over 300 healing crystals (Godsfield Press, 2007)

Good Vibrations: Energy enhancement, psychic protection and space clearing (Flying Horse Books, 2008)

The Crystal Bible, Vols 1, 2 and 3 (Godsfield Press, 2009–2013)

The Book of Why: Understanding your soul's journey (Flying Horse Books, 2010)

The Crystal Experience: Your complete crystal workshop in a book (Godsfield Press, 2010)

Crystal Prosperity: Create Abundance in All Areas of Your Life (Ivy Press, 2010)

101 Power Crystals: The ultimate guide to magical crystals, gems, and stones for healing and transformation (Fair Winds Press, 2011)

The Crystal Healing Pack (Godsfield Press, 2011)

Crystals and Sacred Sites: Use crystals to access the power of sacred landscapes for personal and planetary transformation (Fair Winds Press, 2012)

The Crystal Wisdom Oracle Pack (Watkins Publishing, 2013)

The Crystal Zodiac: Use birthstones to enhance your life (Godsfield Press, 2013)

Crystals to Empower You: Use crystals and the Law of Attraction to manifest abundance, wellbeing and happiness (Walking Stick Press, 2013)

Life-Changing Crystals: Using crystals for abundance, wellbeing and happiness (Godsfield Press, 2013)

Crystals for Psychic Self Protection (Hay House, 2014)

Earth Blessing Crystals: Using crystals for personal energy clearing, Earth healing and environmental enhancement (Watkins Publishing, 2014)

Crystal Prescriptions Volume 2: The A–Z guide to over 1,250 conditions and their new generation healing crystals (O Books, 2014)

Crystal Prescriptions Volume 3: Crystal solutions to electromagnetic pollution and geopathic stress. An A-Z guide. (O Books, reprint edition, 2014)

The stone horoscope: evidence of continuity of ancient esoteric tradition and practice. 'Are an authentic astrological practice and archaic ideological narratives concatenating sky and stones embedded in *The Greek Alexander Romance*?', MA dissertation available on www.judyhall.co.uk

Books by other crystal authors

Gienger, Michael, *Crystal Power, Crystal Healing: the complete handbook* (Cassell, 2002)

Lecouteux, Claude, *A Lapidary of Sacred Stones: Their magical and medicinal powers based on the earliest sources* (Editions Imago, 2011, English trans. Inner Traditions, 2012)

Lilly, Simon, *The Complete Illustrated Guide to Crystal Healing: A step-by-step guide to using crystals for health and wellbeing* (Element, 2011)

Lilly, Simon and Sue, *Crystal Doorways* (Capall Bann Publishing, 1997)

—, *Preseli Bluestone: Healing stone of the ancestors* (Tree Seer Publications, 2011)

Martino, Regina, *Shungite: Protection, Healing and Detoxification* (Healing Arts Press, 2011, translated by Jack Cain)

Temple, Robert, *The Crystal Sun* (Century Books, 2000)

Scholarly sources

Bahler, Ingrid, and Katherine, Gyekenyesi Gatto, *The Lapidary of King Alfonso X the Learned* (University Press of the South, New Orleans, 1997)

Caley, Earle R., and John F. Richards, *Theophrastus on Stones* (The Ohio State University, Columbus, Ohio, 1956)

Evans, Joan, and Mary S. Serjeantson, *English Mediaeval Lapidaries* (The Early English Text Society, Oxford University Press, 1955)

Scalar wave research

Hunt, Valerie, *Infinite Mind: Science of the human vibrations of consciousness* (Malibu Publishing, 1996)
www.valerievhunt.com
www.spiritofmaat.com/archive/jun1/scalar.htm
www.rbduncan.com/sw.htm
www.homeotronics.com

Websites

Robert Coon:
www.librarising.com/esoterica/earthchakras.html

Andrew Lang on crystal balls:
https://ebooks.adelaide.edu.au/l/lang/andrew/making_of_religion/chapter5.html

Ancient sources

Theophrastus on Stones and other ancient and modern sources: www.farlang.com

Cleansers

Clear2Light from www.petaltone.co.uk is an excellent crystal cleanser and is available worldwide. Crystal Charge is also available from Petaltone.

Crystal Cleanser spray from the Crystal Balance Company and Crystal Recharge along with transmuting Violet Flame work wonders: www.crystalbalance.net

Crystal healing organizations and courses

Hay House Basics Crystals online course: I have produced a detailed and easy-to-understand online course to accompany the lessons in this book. You'll see me demonstrate how to work with crystal essences, give crystal healing and learn how to use crystals for divination, besides many other meditations and video lessons. www.hayhousebasics.com

Affiliation of Crystal Healing Organizations: ACHO promotes training and competence in crystal healing therapy and to act as part of the Crystal Therapy Council, which is a member of the General Regulatory Council for Complementary Therapies. ACHO maintains a practitioner register of qualified crystal healers trained to ACHO/CTC standards. www.crystal-healing.org

The Association of Melody Crystal Healing Instructors International: TAOMCHI provides a clearing-house for information concerning instructors and workshops. www.taomchi.com

The Crystal Healing Association of Japan: www.chaj.jp

Crystal Healing and Energy Work Diploma course: The School of Inner Light in Bournemouth, Dorset, and Llandeilo, Wales, offers a unique professional Diploma course in Crystal Healing and Energy Work, which combines crystal therapy/healing, Reiki and vibrational energy work. www.schoolofinnerlight.co.uk/courses/crystalhealingcourse.htm

Sue and Simon Lilly: Online courses in anatomy, colour therapy, crystal therapy, nutrition, physiology and tarot: www.mcscourses.co.uk

Index

ABOUT THE AUTHOR

Judy Hall is an internationally recognized author, crystal expert, astrologer, psychic, healer, broadcaster and workshop leader. She has a BEd in Religious Studies and a Masters Degree in Cultural Astronomy and Astrology, and has an extensive knowledge of world religions and mythology. Her numerous books have been translated into 18 languages.

www.judyhall.co.uk and
www.angeladditions.co.uk

HAY HOUSE BASICS
Online courses

If you're interested in finding out more about the topics that matter most for improving your life, why not take a Hay House Basics online course?

Each course is intended to provide a powerful introduction to a core topic in the area of self-development or mind, body, spirit. Presented by a renowned expert, each course includes:

**An overview of the topic,
including its application and benefits**

•

Video demonstrations of practical exercises

•

Meditations and visualizations to guide you

•

**Specially created text guides, available to
download for future reference**

Available at a special low price, these courses are the ultimate route to a full spiritual life!

Find out more at **www.hayhousebasics.com**

CPSIA information can be obtained
at www.ICGtesting.com
Printed in the USA
FSOW02n0053131214
3838FS